Go to Joseph

Patricio Olmos

Go to Joseph

Meditations with Saint Joseph

Go to Joseph
Meditations with Saint Joseph

Translated by Mariana and Juan Luis Tavella, and reviewed by Fr. Henry Rute

Avenida de Atenas 33
28290 Las Rozas Madrid
(España)

Can be printed. Bishop Hugo N. Barbaro, Bishop of San Roque (Presidencia Roque Saenz Pena, Argentina), March 23, 2021

First edition: October 2021
ISBN: 978-84-17539-51-1
Cover design: BibliotecaOnline SL
Image by Krzysztof Golik window of Saint Joseph, Church saint Ciro and saint Julieta of Canac, Aveyron, Francía. Photo by Tournasol7.
License Creative Commons 4.0 Internacional
Layout: BibliotecaOnline SL
Printed by: Podiprint
Printed in Spain

Index

To Saint Josemaria, thanks to whom I started the wonderful habit of doing days of spiritual retreat every year, and thanks to whom I learned a little of his great devotion to Saint Joseph.

Introduction

Look, I make all things new.
Apocalypse 21:5

Why meditate? Why go on retreat? Why do it with Saint Joseph? For over forty years I have been doing a few days of spiritual retreat every year. At first, it was two or three days, then almost a week. I must confess that I love work, I am interested in what happens in the world and enjoy being with people. And precisely because of this, I feel the need from time to time to call a halt, to get away from the daily routine, step back, to correct the course of my life and regain the enthusiasm that fatigue or poorly faced routines have tended to wear me out. I have always looked forward to those moments of peace and have savored them a lot.

In my years of priestly work, I have preached dozens of retreats of different durations, and I have had the opportunity to talk with those who do it: learning from these people, and intuiting what usually helps - and what does not - in preaching, and in the advices I give in spiritual accompaniment.

There are some basic issues that should always be considered on an extended retreat. But there is the risk of going back on the same issues and approach them without further reflection, as one who repeats without thinking or listens without pondering over them. Therefore, to help me and help my listeners, each year I choose in each retreat a background theme: the Virgin Mary, Saint Peter, Saint Paul, the Transfiguration, the Adoration of the Magi, etc. because, as Saint Paul teaches: in Him, "all the treasures of wisdom and knowledge are hidden" (Col 2:3) and everything that can satisfy our restless hearts. In other words, the theme of each year is a backdrop that allows us to meet Jesus Christ again.

On this occasion, moved by the invitation of Pope Francis to live a year dedicated to Saint Joseph [1], the proposal is to use the Holy Patriarch as an aid. He is a very holy man, who, because of his closeness to the Blessed Mary and her son Jesus Christ, has a great power of intercession. With his figure "so close to our human condition", he is very near to us, ordinary people, who do not stand out in any way, without this fact making our lives lack in importance, like his didn't before God or others.

Anything that can be said to show the exceptional qualities of Saint Joseph is bound to fall short, and on this point I cannot claim any expertise. And so I hope I will be allowed to refer to two excellent works that have served as an inspiration to write these pages: a book by Fr. F. Suarez and a homily by Saint Josemaria Escriva, "At Joseph's workshop" [2]: "For a Christian...,the fact that God chose Joseph to make him the husband of the Virgin Mary and legal father of Jesus is reason enough to think that, after all, he was not such an ordinary and common man when it was God himself who chose him - indeed had created him - to carry out one of the most difficult and most responsible missions that was ever entrusted to any man" [3]. That is the reason why Pope Francis has said that "my predecessors have deepened the message contained in the few data transmitted by the Gospels to highlight his central role in the history of salvation" [4].

With this booklet I would like to transmit the "enthusiasm" I have for retreats and offer some considerations to make them useful, and I hope that at the same time it will serve to increase the readers' devotion to Saint Joseph. Although reference is made here to all the Gospel passages mentioned, it is by no means an attempt to make a biography or history of Mary's husband. These are considerations addressed to those who do a few days of retreat, either based mainly on

---

1 Apostolic Letter, *Patris Corde,* 12-VIII-20.

2 Enclosed in *Christ is passing by*, 39-56; later mentioned as *Joseph's workshop*.

3 F. Suarez, *Joseph, Mary's husband*. Patmos 2006, p. 18-19.

4 *Patris Corde*, Introduction.

this book or as an addition to other reflections they may have had. They are also designed for those who want to pray or do some spiritual reading about the different aspects of the "man who goes unnoticed, the man of the daily, discreet and hidden presence"[5].

I don't necessarily offer new topics; the novelty will be in what each one considers again in the presence of God, even if they already know the life of Joseph or have been on retreats for decades. If there is a new encounter with our Lord, He will shed hope on whoever is looking for him and will strengthen him in his struggle, giving him the possibility of a renewal.

At the beginning of these reflections, I invite you to join the request with which Pope Francis ends his letter on the Holy Patriarch, "There is nothing left but to implore Saint Joseph for the grace of graces: our conversion"

---

5 Id.

Chapter 1
Saint Joseph's silence

But Jesus remained silent.
Matthew 26:53

Inner recollection

The first thing that draws our attention to Joseph is his discreet and attractive silence. No word of his is known. He was the main character and witness of magnificent events, and one would expect some comment or remarks. The Gospels and the Acts of the Apostles collect words from different characters, some made into long speeches, others into short dialogues or phrases. Peter, John, James, Thomas, Judas, Mary Magdalene, Stephen, Paul speak there... even Pilate and Herod have things to say. But not Joseph. Although ultimately it is the Holy Spirit who inspires the evangelists, everything seems to indicate that it is Joseph's proper style.

If his words are unknown, it is not because he had nothing to say, in the sense that he could not think of anything or that he was a laconic person. It might rather be that there was nothing to add to what had already been said. He knew how to be in his place. He was not chosen to witness by speaking, but to watch over Jesus and Mary, and to protect them. His silence is significant and what do we learn from it? What does he teach us who live immersed in so much chatter, and not only on the outside, but also interiorly?

He teaches us not to talk too much and to have that command of the language about which Saint James preaches us in his epistle (cf. 3:1-12). Following Joseph's style, we will not have to give an account to God for foolish or vain words (also those uttered on social networks). He had no need to prove anything to anyone, as can happen to whoever wants to justify himself, or to appear more intelligent, or more knowledgeable. He was at peace with God, he selflessly and diligently fulfilled his mission and he enjoyed it without feeling the need to making himself felt.

What God asked of him, what happened in his life, could have justified on his part an excuse, a complaint or requested an explanation. Nothing of that happened. The enigmas that God created for him by not immediately revealing the cause of Mary's pregnancy or by changing plans to make him flee with his family to Egypt, did not cause any complaint on his part. And not because he was insensitive but rather, thanks to his interior richness of great faith and humbleness, he learned to trust God, who would have his reasons and would communicate them to him when necessary, as in fact happened.

"The most silent person in the Gospel is Saint Joseph, from whom the New Testament does not know a single word. Saint Basil considers silence a condition for our encounter with God" [6].

This serves to underline one of the first requirements that are necessary in order to pray, and more so to make profitably a retreat: silence, with the subsequent recollection.

God speaks quietly

Important things for the soul usually happen during times of reflection and silence. It is the experience we find in the Bible. Thus, Moses will know the name of God and receive his mission to free the Jewish people from Egyptian oppression while he was in the desert of Midian (cf. Ex 3:14). Elijah will recognize the Lord's passage in "the whisper of a gentle breeze", and not in other thunderous phenomena: a hurricane, an earthquake and a fire (cf. 1 R 19:12). John the Baptist will prepare for his significant mission to be the

---

6 R. Sarah, *La fuerza del silencio. Frente ala dictadura del ruido*, Palabra 2017, p. 162.

forerunner of Jesus living in the solitude of the Judean desert. Jesus himself, before the start of his public ministry, dedicates forty days to fasting and silence, in an atmosphere of prayer. And of the great apostle Paul we are told that after his baptism he retired to Arabia (Gal 1:17), from where he came out strengthened for his mission

It is the experience of thousands of Christians throughout the centuries. There were many who were converted or approached God from this practice. For example, Saint Josemaria was doing his spiritual exercises in October 1928 when one morning he "saw" Opus Dei. They were days of silence, in which he was reviewing notes made during previous moments of prayers and he realized what God was asking of him. Sometimes a good part of a successful retreat will be to re-read outstanding notes or resolutions from other retreats.

Doing a retreat is an immense grace. It is a time to be close to God and receive the gifts that He always wants to bestow on us. For this reason, a first invocation should be: "Thank you, my God, because you give me this extended time of prayer"; "I thank you for having brought me here"; "Help me and help us to take advantage of this opportunity"; "Make me tune in with you soon"; "Free me of the worries I have at this moment since it does not make sense that I continue to cling to them: I leave them in the hands of your fatherly providence".

Leaving work or family to take time to pray, could be seen as a disorder. In a letter to a mother of a family, Saint Jerome advised her to withdraw a little from the "family din" in order to pray, read the Bible and meditate", and he ended: "I am not telling you this because I'm trying to make you draw back from your people, what I am rather trying to do is for you to learn and meditate on how you should behave with your people" [7]. Praying is not an act of selfishness, it is really opening up to God, who shows us how to open up to others.

---

7 *Epistle*, 148.

"Solitude is a beautiful thing when you are at peace with yourself and have a definite work to do" (Goethe). And what is a "definite work" these days? In part, being open to what God inspires us: letting ourselves be surprised by the Holy Spirit, who blows where He wishes (cf Jn 3:8). It is not good having everything planned in advance (the themes, the books and, almost, even the resolutions) and leaving no space for divine inspirations... Wishing to know clearly God's plans for us and the means that he grants us to live them is a "beautiful thing".

To know myself and to know God

Apart from the fact of being open to what God wants to show us, we find in an expression of Saint Augustine what should always be present in our prayer, and particularly in a spiritual exercise such as a retreat. "Noverim me, noverim te" [8]. May I know myself and may I know you. The task is to know ourselves and to know God. The task itself is exciting: that we may be able to accomplish it is a different matter

Self-knowledge is not an easy task. It is difficult for us to be objective being the subject of our own life. But whoever tries to beseech divine help will succeed. He will see its lights and its shadows. He will be filled with joy for so many blessings received throughout his life. He will discover the gifted talents and the challenging task involved in developing them and bringing them to their prime. He will also recognize his mistakes and sins, and what remains to be done. And since the fundamental knowledge about who we are is knowing that we are children of God, this certainty will give us a way of facing life as one who knows he is backed by the love of his Father, who shows his infinite love, among other things, understanding our weakness and giving us the strength of his grace. Thus, it is possible to achieve being at

8 "Knowing my and knowing You. That's my prayer", *Soliloquies* 2.1,1.

peace with oneself, which is what Goethe spoke of. To go deeply into this is a beautiful task.

And what about the attempt to get to know God better? God is the greatest of all and holds in Himself an infinite perfection: it is worthwhile getting to know Him! To get close to Him is to get closer to beauty, goodness, truth, joy and to all his perfections. It is a fact that in a period of retreat the preacher will never be perfect, or that the books that are used for meditation will have dense or boring parts, or that effort of paying attention for a long time to various subjects can be tiring. But it is also true that the experience of anyone who has tried these tasks is mostly joyous. How can we not be happy to discover, experience or remember that "God is love" (1 Jn 4: 8)? How is it not going to bring peace to our consciences to contemplate the divine mercy? And so we could continue in relation to so many truths that are meditated on during a retreat.

Recollection is easier on retreat days, although it should not be taken for granted. From time to time, I have met someone who arrives full of good intentions, but does not know how to "cut off" from his work - because - he considers himself indispensable, or because he does not know how to reasonably defend his time from unnecessary demands, and so, when he realizes it, those days are over. It can also happen that someone does not know how to do without his phone with everything it contains. To "connect" with God, you have to know how to "disconnect" from everything else.

Perhaps it can help many people, to favour concentration, to take notes during meditations or classes, at least at the beginning. They will rarely hear brilliant ideas, though sometimes God can give us some. It happens that when we write, our attention span increases a lot. I remember a man who told me with a surprised look: "Taking notes changed my way of participating in retreats".

The blessed loneliness in midst of the noise

From Joseph's silences we can also aspire to achieve better recollection during the year. Life is hectic at times and noisy, and there are situations or professions that coexist with the hassle without there being anything wrong in itself: a large family with small children, a school, driving vehicles in densely populated areas, work in a factory, etc. This is reason enough to seek "daily a few minutes of that blessed solitude that is so necessary to keep the interior life in motion" [9]: to seek the grace of God, to become aware that He is with us, to rectify the intention or to tell him that we love Him. Short whiles dedicated exclusively to dealing with our Lord.

It pays to fight and avoid distraction. Someone spoke of "mental zapping": constantly changing the focus of attention and not having it focused on anything in particular. In this way a poor human relationship does not take long to arrive (people gathered together but each one in his own world, be it a cellphone, a tablet, etc). As a result, the quality of intellectual work -study, reading- is poor. In a book by Cardinal Sarah he gives the example of someone walking through a noisy city with a radio on in his pocket, and not realizing that it was switched on. But if he entered a quiet place, he would notice it right away and try to turn it off. And, he adds "unfortunately, there is no button that lowers the chatter of our imagination" [10]. I think there are many of us who have seen how the proportion of dispersed people, absent from their environment, has grown at the rate of technology and who, because of this attitude, usually have a superficial relationship with God and with others. Perhaps this is our case.

How good it is to be able to speak, to know how to communicate. And how good it is also to know when to keep

---

9 Saint Josemaria. *The way*, 304. As for now the following books by this author will only be mentioned by its name: *Furrow*, *Forge*, *The way*, *Christ is passing by*, and *Friends of God*.

10 Cf. *La fuerza del silencio. Frente a la dictadura del ruido*, Palabra 2017, p. 231.

quiet, for example, so as not to speak all the time about one self. At one point in the book "Furrow", among the obvious faults of humility the author points out the following: "to use in the conversation words of self-praise or that imply your honesty, your wit or skill, your professional prestige..."[11]. This attitude can be a lack of interest in others and, because of how annoying it can be, it is a lack of charity, but also of little benefit to us: whoever does not keep quiet, does not listen, and misses the opportunity of enriching himself with other people's conversation.

With his style, Joseph shows himself to us as a man focused on what is important: Mary and Jesus. Everything else is secondary. With his contemplative attitude, he was able to recognize, to listen to the angel of the Lord, who addressed him four times while he slept. God often speaks in a low voice: may our recollection lead us to hear what God tells us in a subtle but unequivocal manner.

11 N. 263.

Chapter 2
Purity of heart

Mary's husband.
Matthew 1:36

The most chaste husband

When they introduce the Holy Patriarch in their respective Gospels, both Matthew and Luke do so in relation to Joseph's marriage to Mary: "Jacob was the father of Joseph, the husband of Mary, of her was born Jesus who is called Christ" (Mt 1:16); the angel Gabriel was sent to "a virgin betrothed to a man named Joseph, of the house of David, and the virgin's name was Mary" (Lk1:26-27).

Mary and Joseph were true husband and wife, even though they never had marital intimacy. "According to the practice of the Hebrew people, the marriage was carried out in two stages: first the legal marriage (a true marriage) was celebrated and, only after a certain period, the husband brought the wife into his house. Before living with Mary, therefore, Joseph was her husband, but Mary kept in her intimacy the desire to give herself exclusively to God" [12].

Everything seems to indicate that Mary's purpose to remain a virgin was known and accepted by her husband. Their love for each other was sublimated by the love of God and moved by a supernatural motion they had resolved to marry, renouncing the right to their bodies.

The adjective "most chaste" has often been mentioned in spiritual literature alongside the noun "husband". On this point, Pope Francis comments: "It does not merely refer to

12 John Paul II, *Redemptoris Custos*, 18.

a virtuous disposition, but the synthesis of an attitude that expresses the opposite of possessing. Being chaste is being free from the desire to possess in all spheres of life. Only when a love is chaste, it is true love" [13]. Pope Francis also adds: "He never became the center. He knew how to be off-center in order to have Mary and Jesus at the center of his life". Joseph had a great capacity to love, to sacrifice himself for those he loved and to serve them properly. He mainly served God made man - Jesus - and Mary most holy, but there is no doubt that because of his capacity for love with a clean heart he also served all the inhabitants of Nazareth.

It is appropriate to believe Joseph as a young person, of a similar age as Mary. "To live the virtue of chastity, one must not wait to be old or to lack vigor. Purity is born of love, and the robustness and joy of youth are no obstacles to a clean love. The heart and body of Saint Joseph was young when he married Mary, when he learned of the mystery of her divine Maternity, when he lived with her respecting the integrity that God wanted to bequeath to the world, as one more sign of his arrival among creatures. Whoever does not understand such a love, knows very little of what true love is, and he is completely unaware of the Christian meaning of chastity" [14]. Chastity is the virtue that helps to love more and better, therefore it is logical to always see it as something positive and never as a set of useless prohibitions or limitations.

For they shall see God

Although chastity is not the main virtue, it is essential in order to achieve dialogue with God. The clean love of Saint Joseph can help us seek the purification of our soul to make a good retreat, and in a normal way to listen and see God: "Happy the pure in heart, for they shall see God" (Mt 5:8). It is necessary to keep the senses to be able to relate to God.

13 *Patris Corde*, 7.

14 *In Joseph's workshop*.

For example, it has always been necessary to take care of your eyesight, but it would seem that at times when so many things are just a "click" away on the phone or computer, or the visual offer has been increased through dozens of television channels and applications Netflix type, you have to create good habits and not rest on one's laurels because the consequences can be devastating.

We want to see God in a normal way to recognize him in our daily lives. Like Joseph who was regularly contemplating Mary and Jesus, those two great wonders that had been entrusted to him. It is true that from time to time he saw surprising things, such as when the shepherds appeared next to the manger moved by the indication of an angel, or when he saw and heard the reaction of the old Simeon: "His father and mother stood there wondering at the things that were being said about him" (Lk 2:33). But most of the time Joseph did not "see" anything special: he was close to Jesus, first a child and then a young man, always growing, behaving like any other. Despite not perceiving special things, through the purity of his heart he was able to realize the greatness of the mystery of a hidden God, a patient God and a humble God.

When commenting on how the apostle John recognized Jesus during the miraculous fishing that he performed after his Resurrection (cf. Jn 21:1-13). Saint Josemaria reflects: "Then the disciple whom Jesus loved turns to Peter: It is the Lord. Love, love can see from afar. Love is the first to grasp these refinements. The adolescent Apostle, with the strong affection he feels towards Jesus, because he loved Christ with all the purity and all the tenderness of a heart that has never been corrupted, exclaimed: It is the Lord" [15].

Let us ask God to grant us a pure heart, and let us work to shape it like this, with the action of grace, present in the Eucharist, the Confession and the times of prayer. How good it is to be able to recognize the Lord in everyday life. He awaits us in our daily existence, to be more positive or smiling. At

15 *God's friends*, 266.

work, to provide effective service to those with whom we interact. In the unexpected contradiction, so that we can offer a small sacrifice that adds merit to the community of saints.

A THANKFUL LIFE

Joseph was always very appreciative of the gift God gave him of being the husband of Mary and Jesus' guardian. He thus perceived the absolute love and trust God had for him. This love was being progressively increasing during their life together. Surely, in his own way, he would say what Elizabeth said in the presence of Mary in her home: "who am I for the Lord to give me such a gift of living continuously next to the mother of my Lord, next to this wonderful woman. Who am I to be able to offer my services to the Savior who condescended to live in my house". Somehow in a silent manner, he also recited his Magnificat of thanks when considering the great benefits received.

How good it is to recognize the gifts of God: "It is right to give him thanks", as it is said in the Preface of Mass. How much good it does to the soul. It helps to properly focus the vision of our life, often obscured by the daily hustle. When we give thanks for the blessings received, we naturally find a remedy against envy and lack of realism. "How many people would like to be in our place": It is not a phrase of easy consolation, it is a truth that asserts itself when one takes the trouble of opening up to the recognition of how much has been given to us.

A psychologist relates that one day a depressed man came to her consulting room. He was blind and in his forties. After listening to him she gave him the task to writing down the good things that were happening to him. To her surprise, on the next session he brought four notebooks full of positive remarks. And there he mentioned simple things, like the temperature of the shower in the morning, the wonder of using a dry towel, getting into bed with clean sheets, going to bed with clean pajamas, the smell of toast, the sun shining on his face when taking a walk, the smell of jasmine when strolling along, the sparkles of the soda reaching his nose, the courtesy of a cashier in the supermarket, and a very long etcetera. With this thoughtful task he considered himself cured and never felt depressed again [16].

If we seek to have a clean heart, which among other things implies having a grateful heart, we should make a list of the good things that happen to us in our own life. And surely, along with small things like those the blind man in the anecdote valued, we will find numerous others of great significance: family, friends, health in so many good aspects, heritage, faith, training, opportunities in life, and also a long etcetera. It is a good way to start a retreat.

The apostle John, who was so close to Jesus and who calls himself in his Gospel as the "disciple that Jesus loved" could confirm years after the departure of Our Lord: "we have known and believe in the love that God has for us." (Jn 1:4-16). Not only did he believe in the love of God but he knew it, he experienced it. He was aware of how much Jesus had done for him: he chose him to be with him and to send him to preach, he gave him the power to perform miracles, he called him his friend. He took care of his rest by taking him out one day for a walk. But John, above all, knew the love of Jesus when he saw how He put into practice what He preached, "no one has greater love than the one who gives hi life for his friends" (1 Jn 15:13). The same happened to Saint Paul, who was deeply moved by this personal love of Jesus: "And the life that I now live in this body I live in the faith of the Son of God, who loved me and gave his life for me" (Gal 2:20). We are also invited to a similar experience. It is not enough that we are told that God loves people, or that he especially loved this or that saint, we need to go through the personal experience and savor his love. Gratitude is an attitude of the heart that helps to experience the savoring of love that God has for us. We can become aware of it being alone with him.

16 In: https://bit.ly/2NwwiFN

Blessed Alvaro del Portillo said a simple prayer of great wisdom. He addressed Our Lord saying: "Thank you, pardon me, and help me more". He repeated it especially on his personal anniversaries. It is a good way to start a dialogue with God, and a very appropriate way to end the day. For example, while one falls asleep making a brief recount of the day, the "Thank you!" arises naturally. How many good things happened! We should also be able to give thanks for those events that have upset us, because in some way they have been for our good. "Pardon me!". There will be things that, far from filling us with pride, lead us to repentance and, if we share them with God, they will not plunge us into discouragement because we will also feel the kindness of a God who forgives. And "Help me more!". Life goes on, the challenges are in force and we seek your strength to restart the fight. What a good aspiration to repeat in retreats.

Chapter 3
The holiness that God offers us

Whereupon Joseph her husband, being a just man, and not willing publicly to expose her, was minded to put her away privately.
Matthew 1:19

Joseph was a saint

Joseph faced a great dilemma, when he began to perceive that his wife Mary was pregnant [17]. Perhaps he was alerted by comments from relatives and neighbors. He was reluctant to believe those opinions. But over time he had to surrender to the evidence. And there began his suffering. What was he to do, how should he act?

He thought that it was not enough to let events just happen. There were very serious things at stake. He had a choice to make, and the consequences would be significant. He was not the father of the child in gestation, and the Law did not allow him to ignore such a situation. On the other hand, as far as he could understand, that same law told him that he had to disown Mary [18]. But he maintained the certainty of the great holiness of his beloved wife: it did not even cross his mind that she had done something wrong. Rather, he was inclined to think that there was something supernatural involved, in which he was not called to be a part. Therefore, the predicament was great.

17 The subject can be read in more detail in P. Olmos, *Omnia in bonum*, p. 44-45. From now on: *Omnia in bonum*.

18 Cf. Dt 22:20-21.

Joseph thought and prayed constantly. He couldn't get the subject out of his head. But he did not reason as someone without faith, nor as one who seeks firstly his personal interest. In those moments he did not allow himself to be carried away by anger towards God or towards Mary because of what he did not understand and totally exceeded him. The sacred text gives us some precise data: he did not want to expose his wife to infamy and made the decision to abandon her in secret, and both things were preceded by the same cause: he was a righteous man. He looked for a solution that would not harm Mary and he took the negative consequences upon himself. He would be the one to be misjudged, and others, without understanding the situation, were going to show solidarity to her.

What is this justice that characterized Joseph? What is this attitude that guided his will in such a dramatic moment? We want to know it, to learn to solve problems and to imitate such an admired man. Without falling into an erroneous simplification, it is possible to assert that this justice is synonymous with holiness. Thus, Saint Josemaria assures us: "For this reason, the Holy Scripture praises Joseph, affirming that he was a just man. And, in the Hebrew language, just means pious, irreproachable servant of God, doer of the divine will (cf. Gen 7:1), other times it means to be good and charitable towards others (cf. Tob 7:5). In a word, the just man is the person who loves God and shows this love by fulfilling his commandments and positions his whole life in serving others, his brothers" 19. And Suarez simplifies it even more: "He therefore decided to secretly abandon her and by this decision he showed that he was a just man, that is to say a saint" 20. If we wish to imitate Joseph, we must pay attention primarily to his sanctity of life.

Saint Josemaria describes the holiness of Joseph with deep clarity in a simple statement: "He knew how to live each and every one of the events that made up his life as

---

19 *In Joseph's workshop.*

20 *Joseph, Mary's husband,* p. 61.

God wanted" 21. He tuned in to God in such a way that he interpreted everything properly and acted accordingly. Although it may seem naïve to arrive at this quotation, I remember that in my youth I read what Noel Claraso wrote, with a sense of humor, in a book about how to play tennis. There he said: "The most important thing, in each game, is not to lose the ball and return it in such a way that it bounces back on the other side of the net. He who always achieves this will soon be a world champion". Very easy to say, and difficult to achieve. In fact, nobody always succeeds, but whoever comes closest to this ideal wins matches and is crowned as champion. Jokes aside, holiness does not require rare qualities and it is perfectly possible, since in this "match" God is on our side: it is only a matter of behaving as God wants at all times counting on the grace that He gives us and that is superabundant.

We can all be holy

"Paradox: it is more achievable to be holy than wise, but it is easier to be wise than holy" [22]. It is more achievable because God invites all who are baptized to seek this ideal. It is less complicated than we usually think, but it requires total determination. It is achievable because it is God who sanctifies us. Holiness is not a matter of willpower or big effort, but is the work of sanctifying grace. It is a question of counting on the strength of God, of living in such a way knowing that: "I live, not with my own life but with the life of Christ who lives in me" (Gal 2:20). It is allowing grace to enter our lives so that He is the one who acts. "Being saints is not doing more and more things or meeting certain standards that we have set ourselves as a task. The way to holiness, as

21 *In Joseph's workshop.*

22 *The Way*, 382.

Saint Paul explains, consists of complying with the action of the Holy Spirit, until Christ is formed in us" (cf. Gal 4:19)[23].

Holiness is possible because it is God who causes it. We would be wrong to think that it depends mainly on us. Primarily it depends on the Holy Spirit - the Sanctifier - and on "sanctifying" grace. For this reason, he who really wants the holiness that God asks for, seeks to be united to the Eucharist, if possible, with daily Mass and Communion. He does not want to lose the grace of confession, and frequently goes to "sanctify" himself in that sacrament: he hands over to God his sins, which he regrets, and God, making an admirable exchange, grants him sanctifying grace. For this same reason, he also seeks a dialogue in prayer with his Savior.

Someone could reject those statements as incomplete and claim the role of the will of each creature. It is not that this role is being denied, far from it, what we want here is to highlight the role of God in holiness, and in order to achieve it, our will must "board the train of grace", and not fall into the willful reductionism of wanting to do things mainly with one's own strength.

In a retreat, it is appropriate to ask ourselves how we are following the path to holiness which God called us to. Some readers will be aware of some specification that makes the universal call to holiness more concrete: the matrimonial vocation, the priestly vocation, celibacy in the midst of the world, or some institutional commitment. This specific way to seek the fullness of the Christian life provides guidelines on how to live each and every one of the events of one's life, just as the Lord wants. Am I aware that God has chosen me from all eternity to be holy? Do I live with the hope that I will achieve it because for God nothing is impossible and it is He who has chosen me? Am I willing to start over again, right now, to put into practice what God expects of me?

The Lord calls us to holiness because He ultimately wants us to be happy: "I have told you this so that my joy may be

23 F. Ocáriz, *Pastoral letter*, 28.X.2020.

in you and your joy may be complete" (Jn 15:11). Obviously there will be difficulties or afflictions, but perfectly compatible with great joy. And not only at the end of one's life in Heaven, but also during the earthly journey. Many are often affected by the statement that "the happiness of Heaven is for those who know how to be happy on earth" [24]. But it is logical that it should be so, because who is the one who knows how to be happy if not the one who loves and knows himself loved, the one who is grateful, the one who does not constantly complain, the one who learns not to be selfish, the one who struggles to conquer himself, in short, the one who struggles to be holy? Joseph had hard and difficult moments, but what always prevailed was joy: he knew he was loved and favored by enjoying the constant presence of Mary and Jesus.

HOLINESS IN EVERYDAY LIFE

There is another simple and profound definition of holiness. "Do you really want to be a saint? Carry out the little duty of each moment: do what you ought and concentrate on what you are doing" [25]. A program that deserves to examine our conscience to see if we are going that way. The normal duties we face daily show us the path of the divine will. "Carry out the little duty of each moment": for example, if it is Sunday, Our Lord expects me to honor him by going to Mass and resting. But since I am not an isolated being in my rest, He expects me to be charitable, and take the opportunity to visit or accompany that relative or friend I could not visit during the week. Or if it is, say, a Monday, the mother of a family will know what challenges await her, in which God will come out to meet her. "Concentrate on what you are doing": there are diligent ways of approaching the small duties, as well as there are ways of getting rid of them, of falling into such a fulfillment that it degenerates into 'comply and tell

24 *Forge*, 1005.

25 *The Way*, 815.

a lie'. Concentrate on what you are doing leads us to give our best response, to pay the best attention to what we are capable of doing.

I remember what happened to me on a flight with several stops, I had an earache that worsened every time the pressure in the cabin changed. On the first stop, I asked at an information booth for a pharmacy. The person who attended me took the time to ascertain what was wrong with me. After telling him, he suggested that I consult at the airport infirmary. That is where I went. I entered a tiny room staffed by a doctor who spoke little but was very efficient. He gave me two pills and a plastic glass of water, put a little cotton wool in my ears and that was that. These two people who attended me, in a simple and effective way, gave me an example of doing what you ought.

This way carrying out the duty of each moment is an example of the Holy Patriarch. "Joseph in fact, does not seem to have been the type of man who consumes all his efforts, or at least a large part of them, planning projects that are never finished, among other things because they are never started, of that type of man who dreams of large projects and while they take care of them, they let slip the real duty whose fulfillments demand that moment, that duty which is more real than all the wonderful but imaginary constructions in which they tend to be entertained"[26]. He was just, holy, and in each situation he did not avoid doing other than what was really his duty. When he had to think, he thought, when he had to act, he acted, taking into account what had been thought, and what had been prayed. He knew how to improve the present with realism. He found a precarious place for Mary to give birth, and he tidied it up in the best possible way. Was it necessary to leave urgently? He did not hesitate and got them safely to Egypt. And we can assume how much he helped his countrymen with the way he worked: an efficient, predictable, friendly, collaborative, ingenious craftsman.

26 *Joseph, Mary's husband,* p. 274.

It is customary to make resolutions during retreat. They will be put into practice especially when returning to ordinary life. If the reader makes them, do not miss those related to what is truly important, the holiness to which we are called. Each one will know what is best for him. I dare suggest putting more affection in the duties of each day, without neglecting those obligations that the current circumstances demand of him: friendly and positive ways of accompanying a sick family member; review the work schedule, perhaps to arrive on time, but also to leave on time, because the spouse and children are waiting for you; formation or practices of piety. Once a mother of a family excitedly recounted the discovery she had made on her days of retirement about the good she could do to her loved ones with household chores, and she concluded by saying that she had proposed to "cook nicely". For her it was synonymous with showing affection, with making life more pleasant for her loved ones.

Chapter 4
Joseph's prayer

But while he thought on these things.
Matthew 1:20

A man of prayer

Joseph's decision to secretly abandon Mary was not a hasty one. He had been considering what had happened from the perspective that his holiness gave him, "because he was just". For this reason, neither was his conclusion the result of anger or frustration. Important things were at stake. He greatly weighed the great love for his wife; parting with her was extremely painful to him. He was not concerned with his personal interests (his honor, how he would be judged by others; nor his economic situation, because wherever he went, he had to start from zero), but above all what the will of God would be. He was looking for the best way to act, the holiest. And he did it with divine help, asking for light, clarity of mind and heart, in short, the phrase "But while he thought on these things" can be interpreted as "while he prayed".

The few data collected by the Gospels about his life do not speak directly of his prayer. But, in good logic, if we start from "by their fruits you will know them" (Mt 7:16), we can conclude that whoever gave such excellent fruits of holiness was especially united to God: "He who abides in me and I in him, such bears much fruit, because without me you cannot do anything" (Jn 15:6). He must have learned by his harmony with the Blessed Virgin, who kept things pondering them in her prayer (cf. Lk 2:19).

We see him going to the Temple which is a place of prayer. Luke mentions in two occasions: forty days after the birth of Jesus to present him to the Lord (2:22-38), and then when Jesus was twelve years old (2:41-50). With reference to the second visit, we were told that "his parents went to Jerusalem every year for the Passover feast" (2:41). Joseph would not go by mere compliance with the norms: "His fulfillment of God's will was neither routine nor formalistic, but spontaneous and profound. The law that every practicing Jew lived was not for him a simple code or a cold compilation of precepts, but an expression of the will of the living God"[27]. Therefore, he went to the Temple to pray, and that would be his usual attitude.

The silence of Joseph, considered at the beginning of these reflections, with his attitude of recollection, made it easier for him to be in the presence of God and to listen, among so many voices, to the divine. You have to have a special finesse to know how to hear in dreams, and he did it four times.

Gasnier comments on the first announcement of the angel: "He receives the message of God while he sleeps, but that was enough to dispel his fears.... Although the vision had occurred in a dream, there are reasons to believe that it was a vision of prophetic character, without illusion or doubt, which carried in itself the certainty of a divine origin. Joseph was sure that he had not "dreamed" in the usual sense of the term: it is God who has addressed him through an angel"[28].

There was a very particular way of praying for Joseph, and it was the opportunity that he was given to contemplate God made man in Jesus. Except for Mary, nobody could do it like him. It is what this preparatory prayer for Mass recognizes in him: "Oh, happy man, blessed Joseph, to whom it was granted not only to see and hear God, whom many kings wanted to see and did not see, to hear, and did not hear, but also hug him, kiss him, dress him, and protect him". If contemplating is looking thoughtfully, Joseph did it

---

27 *Joseph's workshop.*

28 *Saint Joseph's silences*, p. 75.

during all the time that he lived with that hidden God, and was learning the lessons that this Teacher, from a very young age, was imparting with his humbleness.

Something similar happened to him with the privilege of being so close to the Blessed Virgin. He would share with her so many conversations, most of them stemming from daily life, but there would be no lack of references to the mission of Jesus and the salvation that he would bring. Even though she did not always have answers to some questions, we know that there were things that he did not understand, at least initially (cf. Lk 2:50), his conversation with Mary would always give him peace and hope in God's plans.

THE PRAYER OF THE CHILDREN OF GOD

If we want to achieve the holiness of the holy Patriarch, we must imitate his way of praying. To live the events of our life as God wants, we need to pray. Get close to him, seeking to know what he wants, and trying to accommodate our will and also our sensitivity to his love. This is the best prayer: "Not everyone who says to me: "Lord, Lord" will enter the Kingdom of Heaven, but he who follows the will of my Father who is in Heaven" (Mt 7:21). This was the intention of Joseph's prayer. That is why he had the freedom of movement that allowed him to faithfully follow God's plans: what mattered to him was that divine will which he trusted so much. His prayer anticipated the model that Jesus would later offer us, praying to the Father: "not my will, but yours be done" (Lk 22:42).

It is good to ask for specific things, health, material well-being, apostolic fruits, etcetera. Jesus encouraged us when he said: "ask and it will be given to you" (Mt 7:7), but it is a good prayer as long as the desire to fulfill God's will comes first. In prayer we are going to accommodate ourselves to those designs, not to try to wrestle with him and expect Him to change. Starting from the trust in divine goodness, when the person of faith prays, he seeks to know God's will, and seeks His strength and joy to live it. Ours cannot be a willful or whimsical prayer. It is said that one day a boy asked his father, who had come to pick him up from school, which was the capital of France. His father after replying that it was Paris, asked him why he wanted to know. "I had a test and I wrote that it was Rome". After a while, when passing near his room, the father heard him begging on his knees: "Let it be Rome! Let it be Rome!"

Prayer and ordinary life

Keeping the obvious distance from Saint Joseph, at different times in our lives we all find ourselves faced with dilemmas that we must solve: do I accept a promotion at work that implies partly reducing my attention to the family? What attitude should I take towards my spouse when it has become very difficult to live with her? How should I react to the daughter and her partner who have decided to live together out of wedlock? What do I do with the adolescent son who states that he is not clear about his sexual identity? The right thing to do is obviously to face the problems and reflect on them. Usually, when confronted with matters of a certain complexity, it is not a good practice to let things take their course or let someone else solve them. These things do not necessarily happen because one is bad or has made a mistake. Life is very rich in alternatives and circumstances, and God counts on them for our maturity and gives us the grace to solve them. We are required to exercise the virtue of prudence, which will imply further study, to ask for advice and mainly to pray.

When we stop to think while on retreat, there should be no shortage of questions such as: How has my life of prayer been in recent times? Have I abandoned or neglected a good habit I had or some previous resolution? Do I pray for love and with love or just pray to ease my conscience? It is also essential to make a request related to the way of praying, for example: Lord, teach me to pray. Grant me the grace to improve my life of prayer. May I listen to you and support you, especially in what you want to show me during these days?

The fruit of prayer

"While he was considering these things...", the angel informed him of the divine plans, which to his great joy, consisted in receiving Mary as his wife. Although in the next chapter we will be able to consider about the content of those plans, we now pay attention to the fact that we always obtain some result from a prayer well-done, even though it may not be the one expected. Joseph had resigned himself to do what he believed was the best for Mary; he had decided to make the great sacrifice of leaving her. It was not necessary. Just as it was not necessary for Abraham to sacrifice his son Isaac because the interior sacrifice was enough for God (cf. Gen 22:12), in a similar way God accepted his intimate sacrifice.

Jesus also obtained some fruit from his dramatic prayer before he died. He had asked that, if possible, he should not have to drink the bitter chalice of his Passion, but, as has already been recalled, he accepted the will of his Father. Jesus will finally die on the Cross. Does this mean that the Father did not listen to him? Absolutely not: on the one hand, an angel from heaven consoled him (Lk 22:43), which may mean that God saved him from distress. But, on the other hand, during this prayer he gave to the Father the offering of his life with which he obtained Redemption for us. Finally, we must bear in mind that God resurrected and glorified him [29]. Prayer well done always bears fruit. A well-done prayer is that prayer which is done with the intention of entering into communion with God and loving him, putting into practice his inspirations. Praying in this manner implies faith, hope, love of God and humbleness, and that is why it is always effective. It is compatible with the fact that one day there

29 *Catechism of the Catholic Church*, n. 2606.

may not be much desire to pray or that one spends the time fighting against distractions.

The resolutions of a few days of spiritual retreat should include one related to our prayer: on how to do it, on the dispositions that should be emphasized (faith, docility, perseverance...) or on things as definite as those suggested by saint Josemaria [30]: "Practice meditation for a fixed period and at a fixed time -- Otherwise we would be putting our own convenience first: that would be a lack of mortification. And prayer without mortification is not at all effective." On the other hand, at a meditation preached in 1955 to those who were doing an annual retreat, he told them, with the proper tone of his preaching: "If you end up with the firm resolution of trying to live a life of prayer, of trying to seek having a loving conversation with the eternal Love, I assure you, that you will become what the Lord wants of you: a soul that gives him comfort and is effective at the time of doing apostolate" [31].

Resolutions during prayer

As soon as Mary's husband heard the angel's message in his prayerful sleep, he made decisions. "When he woke up, Joseph did what the angel of the Lord had ordered him to do", and without hesitation he "received his wife" (cf. Mt 1:24). He did the same when the angel told him that they should flee to Egypt. It is the same decisive style of Mary when listening to the archangel Gabriel. Her "be it done unto me according to Your Word", generous and available to God is accompanied by the determination to go and serve Elizabeth. The message did not directly mention that she should take care of her. But she registered the fact that her elderly relative was pregnant, pondered it and consequently decided to go there in a hurry (cf. Lk 1: 36-39).

---

30 *Furrow*, 446.

31 *In dialogue with the Lord*, n. 2.

Jesus ends his prayer in Gethsemane with these words to his apostles "Get up, let's go" (Mt 26:46). He had prayed, he had offered himself, he had received more consolation from the angel than from the apostles, and thus he could face his painful Passion.

Often in prayer we will make the decision to change something that we must improve, or do something specific that we have been delaying. If we have already made the great decisions of our life (follow the Lord closely, assume our own vocation), it will usually be small decisions but of great benefit: going to confession, smiling more, getting ready to play with young children, taking up the pending and cumbersome task with new courage, or helping someone specific.

Teacher of interior life

In addition to helping and interceding for those who appeal to him, a saint like Joseph can teach a very particular science, the science of the interior life. "Saint Joseph really is a father and lord. He protects those who revere him and accompanies them on their journey through this life - just as he protected and accompanied Jesus when he was growing up. As you get to know him, you discover that the holy patriarch is also a master of the interior life - for he teaches us to know Jesus and share our life with him, and to realize that we are part of God's family"[32]. He tells us of his closeness with Jesus and also with Mary.

It is essential to learn the science of prayer. The author of "The Way" goes to a great authority on the subject to encourage people to go to the Holy Patriarch. "Speaking of Saint Joseph in the book of her life, Saint Teresa says: 'Whoever fails to find a Master to teach him how to pray

32 *In Joseph's workshop.*

should choose this glorious Saint, and he will not go astray' - This advice comes from an experienced soul. Follow it"[33].

It is common to find feelings of joy and peace among those who make a retreat. It is enough to have some knowledge of the Gospels, to be able to identify oneself with Peter on the Thabor mountain: "It is wonderful for us to be here". It is good to know that these same feelings can be extended throughout the year if they are encouraged in prayer and inner recollection, according to one's own possibilities.

---

33 *The way*, 567.

CHAPTER 5
DISCOVERING AND DEVELOPING YOUR VOCATION

Do not be afraid to receive Mary, your wife.
Matthew 1:20

THE KIND LIGHT OF THE VOCATION

Joseph's great doubt was cleared one day, while sleeping. An angel of the Lord told him what was happening with Mary, and also let him know his own vocation, what God had in mind for him. "Joseph, son of David, do not be afraid to receive Mary, your wife, because what has been conceived in her is the work of the Holy Spirit. She will give birth to a son, and you must name him Jesus, because he is the one who is to save his people from their sins" (Mt 1:20-21). God thought of him so that he would receive Mary and to name the one who was the fruit of the Holy Spirit. He was called to be the guardian of the greatest treasures that would inhabit this world: Mary and Jesus. He was being invited to contemplate closely the most sublime holiness: God made man and the holiest of creatures.

He was not to be a mere spectator. As events developed, it will be seen that he required great qualities. "Joseph is not a man who passively resigns himself. He is a brave and strong protagonist" [34]. He will put himself entirely, without reservation at the service of the mission entrusted to him, also using all his qualities, which were not few.

With this vocation, his joy crystallized. From that moment on he knew certainly how God was counting on him. He

34 Pope Francis, *Patris Corde*, 4.

had been chosen to be with Mary, his wife! and he could collaborate with the Redemption, nothing more and nothing less than receiving as a father the Messiah who had been miraculously conceived without his intervention. As time went by and through the difficulties that he encountered and overcame, such a joy was increased.

The church liturgy takes a few words from Jesus to summarize his life: "The Lord has put his faithful servant in charge of his household" (Lk 12:42). He was in charge of his house, of his family, of God's family, and he completely fulfilled that role. He knew how to protect Mary and her dignity: what would have been a single mother in those days? Wouldn't her son have had a stigma of dishonor? Initiatively obeying civil laws, he went to Bethlehem, and thus brought about the fulfillment of the prophecies regarding Jesus's birthplace. He provided the means for him to be circumcised, and named him Jesus, just as the angel had indicated. He took him at a suitable moment to the Temple, so that he could be presented to the Lord. He also developed the best of his creativity to protect his own from Herod's cruelty. Later, with great affection he provided for the growing up and education of Jesus.

Example of loyalty

Like so many others, Saint Josemaria finds in him an example of fidelity to his vocation. "Joseph's self-giving is an interweaving of faithful love, loving faith, and confident hope. His feast is thus a good opportunity for us to renew our commitment to the Christians calling God has given each of us" [35]. He would surrender, without reservation, through real acts of love, faith and trust. How inspiring is the example of the Holy Patriarch to review how we live our mission in a usual way! Following his example, we must appreciate the gift God

35 *In Joseph's workshop.*

has given us by developing the talents that we have at the service of our journey.

The vocation of every Christian is a source of great joy. Ultimately, it is always a call to love. How can we not be happy to know that God loves us? A person who has a vocation to get married, how could he not be very happy to discover that his love is reciprocated? And it is clear that this has to do with his vocation.

What a shame if someone understood or assumed his mission in life with a fatalistic sense! "I do it because I have no alternative, but if it was left to me, I would run away". It seems to me that if that were the case, that person would not have understood the goodness and providence of a God who wants the best for us. On the contrary, "our calling discloses to us the meaning of our existence. It means being convinced, through faith, of the reason for our life on earth. Our life, the present, past and future, acquires a new dimension, a depth we did no perceive before. All happenings and events now fall within their true perspective: we understand where God is leading us, and we feel ourselves borne along by this task entrusted to us" [36]. It is as if the pieces of a puzzle began to fit together: parental love, educational opportunities, childhood difficulties, changes of address, that illness, that friendship, that facility for...

With a vocation the meaning of our existence is illuminated, the mission that we have and will have until the end of our lives: it is not something temporary! Transitory will be certain circumstances that with the passage of time will change, but what is essential will always remain.

Someone can develop for several years an intense activity in favor of his family and the church, making a visible apostolate: he takes care of the Christian formation of his children and friends; he gives formative talks to different groups of people; he takes on a job that, in addition to being his source of income, gives him prestige and a place in

36 *In Joseph's workshop.*

society. But time goes by and the strengths are decaying. Not only the children have left home, the parental home, but the moment of retirement has come. The temptation of sadness, the feeling of emptiness and worthlessness could ensue. And now what? my life doesn't make sense? Of course it makes sense! but in a different way. God is faithful. Whoever called us once continues to call us without ever abandoning us. Essentially, He invites you to the same thing: to love him above all things and to love our neighbors. Perhaps the time has come to serve God with more rectitude of intention, without so much "liking" or affective return for what is done. To realize even more that one is only an instrument and that it is God who gives the increase (cf.1 Cor 3:6). It is the opportunity to pray more, to offer sacrifices previously unthinkable, to move forward with a joyful fidelity that will be an encouragement and example for others, although they will not necessarily have to recognize it that way.

"And me, what do I live for?"

One Sunday morning, very early, I was going to celebrate mass. A young man looking like he was returning from a party, when he saw me, he asked me without any introduction: "And me, what do I live for?" Beyond the answer that I tried to give him in midst of my surprise, he has always remained as a figure of the question that sooner or later we all ask ourselves. It is not just one more question, important things depend on the answer we give, including happiness itself. This boy sensed the importance of getting right the "why" and "for what" of our life.

By the grace of God, many of us are already clearly aware what we live for, but that does not mean that we may frequently ask ourselves that question again, to have even clearer the details of the path we continue to follow. Joseph would repeat himself in some way: "I live for God, who entrusted me to take care of Mary and Jesus". In this he found the illusion of getting up every morning, of living with his loved ones and of facing his daily work. God grant us to be clear about why we live. If we ask, we will be faced with the typical request that will not go unanswered. I don't know what will happen if someone asks God he wants to win the lottery, but how can he not agree to the request to show what he wants from each one?

We all have a vocation. God loves us uniquely and counts on each one of us. Pope Benedict XVI said it beautifully at the beginning of his pontificate: "We are not the casual and meaningless product of evolution. Each one of us is the fruit of a thought of God. Each one of us is loved, each one is necessary" [37]. First of all, we discover that we are loved and needed by realizing the universal vocation to holiness: "Because this is the will of God: your sanctification" (1 Thessl 4:3). "He chose us before the creation of the world so that we would be holy and without blemish in his presence, for love" (Eph 1:4). But that same vocation becomes more specific: seeking holiness in marriage, in celibacy, in the priestly order, etc.

Contemplating Joseph's loyalty to his vocation, the question also arises about the fidelity to ours. Federico Suarez comments: "Nothing diverted Joseph from the path that had been drawn out for him. No obstacle, no threat, no danger could break, or even lessen, his loyalty. Nor did he give in to the temptation -too easy, at times- of the ambition to climb, to be more, that kind of slippery slope by which, in a barely noticeable way and under a layer of higher performance, you can end up justifying the lack of loyalty on the pretext of being in a position to provide a more effective service. Joseph was a man who remained in his position and subordinated all legitimate ambition to the mission entrusted to him" [38]. Do I take care of my vocation as something central in my life, something that unifies everything else? Do I appreciate it as a treasure that it really is? Have I known how to be delicately

37 *Homily*, 24-IV-2005.

38 *Joseph, Mary's husband*, p. 275-276.

faithful, even when things got difficult? What aspect of my dedication could shine better?

Lukewarmness: a half love

When, on retreat days, or on other occasions, one makes a balance of one's own life, it seems appropriate to ask oneself about fidelity to one's own vocation. Thus one makes sure that one is following the right path, and in the right direction. Because the most frequent danger is not erring the path but the way in which it is traveled. You can have the right family (which is not synonymous with perfect), the right job (which will never be perfect) and you can also have found your place in the church, but if you lack love, if you search for yourself, if you have fallen into lukewarmness or fell into a "burgeois" way of life, neither will it please God nor will He be content with you.

Perhaps the examination of conscience can pass through one of the characteristics of every call: joyful fidelity. Because fidelity is not primarily enduring or resisting. Sometimes it will be necessary to do it like that but, primarily, it is about developing the entrusted task making other people happy, through your service, your company or your presence. Do I usually think of others? What do others think or say about my charity for them? What precise things do they reproach me? What should I change?

The attitude of half-loving did not occur in Joseph's life. "Joseph is surprised and astonished. God gradually reveals his plans to him, and he tries to understand them. As with every soul who wishes to follow Jesus closely, he soon discovers that here is no laggard's pace, no room for the half-hearted. For God is not content with our achieving a certain level and staying there. He doesn't want us to rest on our laurels. God always asks more: his ways are not the ways of men. Saint Joseph, more than anyone else before or since, learned from Jesus to be alert to recognize God's wonders, to have his mind and heart awake"[39].

Taking Joseph as an example whose happiness is in the logic of love, Pope Francis points out to those whose vocations are badly lived: "Every true vocation is born from the gift of oneself, which is the maturation of simple sacrifice. Also the priesthood and consecrated life require this type of maturity. When a vocation, whether in married life, in celibacy or virginity, does not reach the maturity of self-giving, stopping only in the logic of sacrifice, then instead of becoming a sign of the beauty and joy of love runs the risk of expressing unhappiness, sadness and frustration"[40]. Whoever assumes his vocation with true love and self-forgetfulness lives happily, makes those around him happy, and enjoys life. Like everyone else, he will have his difficulties, but they do not frustrate God's call to happiness.

It is also possible to fall into a "burgeois" way of life in marriage. Over time, if someone has not patiently exercised himself in cultivating love for his spouse, he runs the risk of his love fading away. Small egotism tend to stagnate if you are not attentive. Interests revolve more and more around material well-being (outings, meals, electronic devices, excessive care of the body). And the small virtues that make manners gentle and pleasant are neglected: good humor, affability, the indulgence that tends to judge people favorably without dwelling on their defects and mistakes, gratitude, etc.. If this cooling down of charity is not remedied in time, there are estrangements, even attacks, sometimes irreparable.

On the other hand, I have known many couples in love whose love has not been affected by the passage of time. For example, an acquaintance comes to mind who, at one hundred years old, kept giving his wife the red roses for their wedding anniversary that she liked. A small detail but one that was a reflection of his love expressed in a full life, with lots

39 *In Joseph's workshop.*

40 *Patris Corde*, 7.

of children, grandchildren, great-grandchildren, friends and lots of projects carried out throughout his long existence. He had a lot of courtesy, which was undoubtedly possible due to his intense interior life; by the way his name was also Joseph.

Chapter 6
The poverty of Bethlehem

He set out... to...Bethlehem... with Mary, his betrothed, who was with child.
Luke 2:4-5

There was no place for them

Saint Luke tells a story that we will have heard many times, but as it is God's Word, "alive and effective" (cf. Heb 4:12), it always contains a potentiality of grace, allowing us to continue to benefit from it as many times as we approach it. "At this time Caesar Augustus issued a decree for a census of the whole world to be taken" (Lk 2:1-7). This story takes place after telling us of the virginal conception of Mary and the birth of John the Baptist while Quirinius was governor of Syria. It is pointed out that, as the people were going to carry out the census in their city, "Joseph, since he was of David's house and line, set out from the town of Nazareth in Galilee, to the town of David, called Bethlehem, in Judea, in order to be registered together with Mary, his betrothed, who was with child".

The distance between Nazareth and Bethlehem is about one hundred and twenty kilometers, which at that time would be equivalent to a journey of about four to five days. The usual iconography represents this image including a donkey, thus making the trip a little more bearable for his wife. "While they were there the time came for her to have her child, and she gave birth to a son, her first-born. She wrapped him in swaddling clothes, and laid him in a manger because there was no room for them at the inn". It is not possible to say in a simpler and more synthetic way what happened, and behind such a concise narrative there hides much meaning. When praying the Rosary, let us be careful not to hurry in order to better contemplate this mystery in which we must always delve.

It is quite possible that our saint's contemporaries were not pleased with this edict. They could feel humiliated by the Roman emperor and conqueror: he wanted to count them for financial purposes. But we now see Joseph, who would also have his national pride, obeying a human law, which will serve to fulfill the prophecy of Micah: "And you Bethlehem, in the land of Judah, you are by no means least among the leaders of Judah, for out of you will come a leader who will shepherd to my people Israel" (5:1).

There things were not easy. If Joseph risked to make this trip despite Mary's condition, it is because he expected something else: to find accommodation in a lodging, or be welcomed at the home of a relative. It has been explained that such shelters or inns "consisted of a courtyard surrounded by high walls. In the center of which most of the time there was a cistern; around which the beasts would gather, camels that emit a kind of typical roar and braying donkeys. Attached to the wall were some sheds where travelers accommodated their beds. They were often divided by partitions forming compartments, so that between the pilasters were independent enclosures which were offered to the guests" [41]. This more private enclosure is what seems to have been lacking and therefore the minimum conditions of privacy for Mary to give birth were not given, and as a result...: "there was no place for them".

They had what was important

But how do you go from the lack of a suitable place to a manger for animals? It's easy to imagine because worse is

41 F. M. William, mentioned in *Joseph, Mary's husband*, p. 100-101.

having nothing. It was either by indication of some inhabitant of the area or by investigation made by Joseph, that they found a place - stable or cave - that had the trough for the beasts and that could be used as a cradle when God entered the world. Joseph "undoubtedly would not have liked that Jesus should be born in a place that he would never have thought of: a stable for animals. As a good craftsman it would hurt his professional pride not to be able to offer him a cradle at that time, but a manger, something that down the centuries we have covered with poetry, but that clearly no mother would choose for her baby, unless that is better than the hard ground"[42]. Faced with her logical anxiety, Mary would not only console him, but would also see the unique greatness of the moment they were living: Jesus, the Savior, would be born, and this was what was truly important: the circumstances of scarcity and helplessness were secondary. Therefore, he would share the great joy with Mary by overlooking so many annoyances and humiliations and by offering them to God.

When we meditate on the circumstances of Jesus's birth, the one that most attracts our attention is that this was so because of God's choice: Christ wished to be born so; it was not out of negligence on the part of his father, nor because it was "his lot", nor because there was no way out. Voluntarily "being rich, he became poor", to enrich us (cf. 2 Cor:8-9). With this birth he starts a "method" that will be the same up to the Cross, and therefore of his entire earthly existence: poverty and humility.

POVERTY AND WORK

Joseph was immersed in that logic of God since before the arrival of the Child. He was of modest economic condition, had little and worked abundantly. "Joseph was, we have said, a craftsman from Galilee, just one man among many. What

42 *Omnia in bonum*, 47.

had life to offer to someone from a forgotten village like Nazareth? Nothing but work: work every day with the same constant effort. And at the end of the day, a poor little house in which to rest and regain energy for the next day" [43]. He neither could nor wanted the luxury to loaf around. He did not disown his condition.

His detachment from material goods was that of the father of a family who with his work had to support his family, that is why he would charge for his work. "Sometimes, in the case of people poorer than himself, Joseph would charge only a little - just enough for his customer to feel that he had paid. But normally he would charge a reasonable amount - not too much or too little. He would demand what was justly owed him, for faithfulness to God cannot mean giving up rights which in fact are duties. Saint Joseph had to be properly paid, since this was his means of supporting the family which God had entrusted to him" [44]. God did not ask him for what centuries later the monks would experience - an absolute detachment and seclusion from the world - but his was a real poverty, full of small details.

"Blessed are the poor in spirit, for theirs is the Kingdom of Heaven" (Mt 5:3). Christian poverty is not a sociological condition but an authentic virtue; it gives freedom and ease of movement to those who assume it. It leads to having the heart focused on what is important and not getting entangled in attachments that actually impoverish. In the case of the Nazareth artisan, this attitude he always lived "because he was just" is also reflected in his readiness to accept God's plans and his apparent changes. And thanks to this attitude he never seems to lose his humor or get angry.

43 *In Joseph's workshop.*

44 *In Joseph's workshop.*

A BUNDLE AND THE "LIGHT CAVALRY"

It is clear that we are not angels and that due to our human condition we must use material things. Everything works well when we consider them as means and not ends in themselves. When they are received and used in an appropriate manner, it is possible to enjoy their goodness, while one sanctifies oneself by thanking the Creator and administering them for the benefit of his family and society: how many times have we thanked God for some of the technological instruments of recent times, for example: a telephone or a tablet that allows us to have practically the entire Library of Alexandria at our disposal. The problem begins at the moment in which those things that were initially convenient or necessary, with the passage of time and the change of circumstances become superfluous and even harmful.

In the movie "The Mission", Roland Joffe, 1986, there is a scene in which one of the characters in search of penance is dragging a bundle with all his belongings, even climbing a mountain with it. He suffers incredibly and looks exhausted. Finally, after a moment of dramatic uncertainty, he is released when they cut the rope holding the bundle. Then the actor shows so much joy with this liberation, that he transmits it to others. Although in this case the director seems to focus on the liberation that forgiveness of guilt entails, it is also possible to relate it to the weights, more or less conscious of being attached, lacking in temperance, to material things through excessive use.

Perhaps we have seen people who complicate their lives with things they do not need. Pope Francis explained it thus: "Accumulating goods only burdens and inexorably slows down the journey! Here I think of an anecdote: the Spanish Jesuits used to describe the Society of Jesus as the *"light brigade of the Church"*. I remember when a young Jesuit was moving and while he was loading a truck full of his many possessions, suitcases, books, objects, and gifts; an old Jesuit standing by was heard to say with a smile: And this is *"the light brigade of the Church"*? Our moving can be a sign of this disease" [45].

Sometimes we go unnecessarily loaded. To avoid this, it may be good to ask oneself in what or in whom do I have my hopes and illusions. When our hope and longings for happiness are set on God and in fulfilling his will, it may be easier not to covet inordinately well-being and material prosperity. If what fills my heart day after day is to carry out the mission, the vocation that has been granted to me, I will be able to direct everything towards that goal. But if my security is based on what I have and what reflects my status, my image, or is in not messing things up and living peacefully, I am leaning on fragile and slippery bases. Fears and sorrows will come more frequently, because we will be more vulnerable to everything that demands generosity or sacrifice, and we can also incur in comparisons that are harmful.

Whoever wants to develop the call to the apostolate received Baptism, needs to live this Christian virtue that leads us to place our expectations and longings in God above all things. Thus he will not let his apostolic zeal diminish. "Detach yourself from the goods of the world. Love and practice poverty of spirit which enables you to live a simple and sober life. If not, you will never be an apostle!" [46]. Thus the Pope joked about the "light cavalry", I once overheard in a talk that if this virtue was not lived, it was easy to go from the absorbing wish to "change the world" to the equally intense desire of wanting to change the cellphone or the computer.

And what is a necessity for individuals is also necessary for the Church and the world, with its various institutions. For example, regarding integral ecological themes - the care of the common home, which is the Earth-, the last Popes have warned about the risks of insatiable consumerism and have encouraged a change of style in the lives of individuals and

---

45 *Speech to the Roman curia*, 22-XII-2014.

46 *The Way*, 637.

communities, searching for a way of life characterized by soberness and solidarity. "The emptier a person's heart is, the more he needs objects to buy, possess and consume"[47].

Sense of responsibility

Joseph would live his work with the awareness of being the user of talents he had and to put them at the service not only of his Holy Family, but of his fellow citizens, the inhabitants of Nazareth. He had no confused ambition, he worked hard, charging reasonably for his labor, and often accommodating himself to the need of others. He would stick to a work schedule, but if he needed to stay longer because of a neighbor's emergency, he would do it naturally. And if it was necessary to attend to Mary or Jesus, he would know how to dedicate more time to them, as well as "he knew how to take a few days" to be closer to God, for example, once a year for his pilgrimage to the Temple (cf. Lk 2:41). Really he was not attached to his work.

The Servant of God, Enrique Shaw (1921-1962), was an Argentine businessman whose canonization process is advancing. Endowed with great generosity, from a young age he felt an impulse to evangelize the working class, so much so that at some point he seriously considered becoming a worker himself, despite coming from a wealthy family and being a Navy officer. While spending a training period in the United States, he had these reflections and met a priest who prudently redirected his concerns so that he would be a businessman with a Christian outlook. When he left the Navy, he spent his time in raising his large family and taking care of the family's businesses by running a glasswork factory. There he earned the respect and affection of his many employees, who noticed that he loved them not only because of their

47 Pope Francis, *Laudato si*, 204.

work, but also taking care of their problems and families to the best of his ability[48].

When considering the poverty in which Joseph lived, along with Jesus and Mary, the opportunity arises to contrast our behavior in the light of the manger. I remember a priest who, following the first gestures and statements of Pope Francis about the desire for a more spiritual and poorer church, asked himself: "Is it reasonable to have the car I use?" In the light of the manger, one may wonder about the extraordinary expenses that he intends to incur. Sometimes he will be confirmed in doing them, because he has purified his heart and he is not moved by vanity or comfort. But on other occasions he will see clearly that they are not necessary. And he will not feel unhappy, but he will be able to savor the aforementioned promise of Jesus: "Blessed are the poor..."

48 Cf. Ambrosio Romero Carranza, *Enrique Shaw y sus circunstancias,* Buenos Aires, (2005) p. 46. There are also more testimonies about the sense of responsibility of this lay person in: Sara Shaw de Critto, *Viviendo con alegría*, Claretiana (2017).

Chapter 7
The charity of the Holy Family

And they found Mary, Joseph and the Child.
Luke 2:16

To Joseph's love a child was born

Jesus came to this earth in a simple way, unnoticed by the world. However, God did not want his birth to be totally ignored, and for this he sought some witnesses. He could have looked for them, among the wise men of the time or the "experts" in religion in Jerusalem. Following his method of the poor and humble, he invited some shepherds to witness the first hours of his life. According to Luke's account, "In the countryside close by there were shepherds who lived in the fields and took it in turns to watch their flocks during the night. An angel of the Lord appeared to them and...said: "Do not be afraid. Listen, I bring you news of great joy, a joy to be shared by the whole people. Today in the town of David a savior has been born to you: he is Christ the Lord. And here is a sign for you: you will find a baby wrapped in swaddling clothes and lying in a manger" (cf. Lk 2, 8-20). Along with the first and great amazement of the appearance of an angelical creature, a reassuring message came to them: there was nothing to fear, and something very joyful was communicated to them: the birth of the Savior. To corroborate this, "suddenly... with the angel there was a throng of the heavenly host, praising God and singing: "Glory to God in the highest heaven and peace to men who enjoy his favor".

It is not possible to know how much these shepherds understood - theologically speaking - but it is clear that they went to Bethlehem and were amazed. "When the angels had gone from them into heaven, the shepherds said to one another: Let's go to Bethlehem to see this thing that has happened which the Lord has made known to us. So they hurried away and found Mary and Joseph, and the baby lying in the manger. When they saw the child they repeated what they had been told about him, and everyone who heard it was astonished". They did not find fault to the indication received, and thanks to their simplicity they were able to believe that "the Savior, who is the Christ, the Lord" was that child resting in a manger, and they knew how to communicate adequately what they had seen and heard.

Leaving the reflections on humility and simplicity for another moment, we can focus on the fact that the shepherds who obeyed the voice of the angel saw before their eyes a family: "Mary, Joseph and the child", a mother, a father and a son. Although Joseph was not the biological father, he was so in all other respects. Once the Gospels establish the virginal conception of Mary, they have no qualms about speaking of him as his father, without any qualification (legal, putative, adoptive). And so Luke says that Simeon "came to the Temple, and when the parents entered with the child Jesus..." (2:27); "his parents went every year to Jerusalem..." (2:32); and Mary herself will say to Jesus when she finds him after three days: "Look how your father and I looked for you in anguish" (2:48). When showing the genealogy of the Lord, he will say: "Jesus, at the beginning was about thirty years old and he was, it was believed, the son of Joseph (3:23). And at the beginning of public life, he records the incredulous comment of his countrymen: "Is not this the son of Joseph" (4:22).

Knowing how just and how holy he was, it is easy to understand the great affection with which he received Jesus in his life. Since holiness has to do with the fullness of charity, someone as holy as he was must have overflowed with love and affection. He began to love him with all his might even before he was born, and then he lived for Him and his mother.

In a wide sense, fatherhood is not only bringing children into the word, but having towards them the affection and responsibility of a good father. For this reason, Saint Augustine affirms of Joseph: "The fatherhood coming from his heart is better shown by him than by any biological father". "With the heart of a father is how Joseph loved Jesus"[49], that is the title with which Pope Francis starts his Josephine exhortation stressing the different ways in which he was a father to Jesus: a loving father, a father in tenderness, in obedience, in his welcome, in creative courage, in work and in the shadow. He also uses a bold expression, when he says that "Jesus saw God's tenderness in Joseph"[50], and he justifies it with a psalm: "As a father feels tenderness for his children, so the Lord feels tenderness for those who fear him" (Ps 103:13).

Charity with works and truth.

Joseph put all his ability and all his affection at the service of God to care for the family entrusted to him through thick and thin. Most of his days were normal, although he felt the weight of fatigue and the difficulties of each moment. He, too, went through situations of pain and anguish. Not for a minute did he spare his dedication to protect and make happy those whom God had entrusted to him. "Joseph loved Jesus as a father loves his son, giving him all the best that he had. Joseph, taking care of that Child, as he had been ordered, made Jesus a craftsman: he passed on his trade. That is why the neighbors of Nazareth will speak of Jesus, calling him interchangeably "faber and fabri filius": craftsman and son of the craftsman"[51].

The Holy Patriarch, in a very close relation with Mary, was educating Jesus, enabling with his tasks the two statements Luke would make: "The child was growing and becoming strong, full of wisdom, and the grace of God was in him" (2:40), and "Jesus grew in wisdom, in age and in grace before God and men" (2:52). He was taught as every infant: to eat,

---

49 *Patris Corde*, 1.

50 *Patris Corde*, 2.

51 *In Joseph's workshop.*

to speak, to dress, to help with the duties of the house, to interact with neighbors and relatives, to write, to collaborate in the workshop and then learn his trade.

An important part of his learnings had to do with teaching him to pray and know the Scriptures: "As we know, the Gospel has not recorded any of Joseph's words: his is a silent and faithful patient and hard-working presence. We may imagine that he too, like his wife and in close harmony with her, lived the years of Jesus' childhood and adolescence savoring, as it were, his presence in their family. Joseph fulfilled every aspect of his paternal role. He must certainly have taught Jesus to pray, together with Mary. In particular Joseph himself must have taken Jesus to the Synagogue for the rites of the Sabbath, as well as to Jerusalem for the great feasts of the people of Israel. Joseph, in accordance with the Jewish tradition, would have led the prayers at home both every day- in the morning, in the evening, at meals - and on the principal religious feasts. In the rhythm of the days he spent at Nazareth, in the simple home and in Joseph's workshop, Jesus learned to alternate prayer and work, as well as to offer God his labor in earning the bread the family needed"[52].

What an astonishing mystery the annihilation of God who wished to be educated! And what a grace that of his father, who had the great joy of collaborating with this task! How many thanks would this virginal father often give for being called to cooperate with Jesus.

Saint Josemaria wondered: "What must Joseph have been, how grace must have worked through him, that he should be able to fulfill this task of the human upbringing of the Son of God?", and he came to the conclusion that "Jesus must have resembled Joseph in his way of working, in the features of his character, in his way of speaking. Jesus' realism, his eye for detail, the way he sat at the table and broke bread, his preference for using everyday situations to

52 Benedicto XVI, *Public audience*, 28-XII-2011.

give doctrine - all this reflects his childhood and the influence of Joseph"[53].

He was a good father and educator, because he gave all of what he was and had, and because in his piety he wanted to know everything relating to the will of God. Surely we can learn from his charity and his generous and responsible dedication to others, and particularly parents could entrust themselves to him and be inspired by his example.

To love someone is to protect him

Joseph had to use extraordinary means when it was necessary to flee to Egypt. The child's life was in danger. Charity leads - no doubt - to protect those you love from physical and external dangers. But it is also extremely necessary and customary to protect their souls. For example, with young children, enabling them to receive a good formation: educating them in moral virtues, helping that they receive the first lessons of the faith. And when they grow up, depending on their situations, it will be necessary to ensure that this faith can take root and bear fruits.

Until he reaches maturity every son is like a newly converted, a neophyte (from the Greek, neo = "new", and phyton = "vegetable") like a new little plant. And just as crops need protection from the climate and pests, those children require clarity of ideas, guidance and security when facing doubts, confusion, or the influence of the anti-values that they will receive from their friends and the dominant culture. A good father and a good mother are not naïve. Yes, they give their children freedom, but they do not unnecessarily expose them to storms or harmful influences. Some may get their children to be educated in schools with a Christian orientation, (truly sometimes, to achieve this they will have to make financial sacrifices, because these schools will not always

53 *In Joseph's workshop.*

be the cheapest or will be just around the corner). But those parents, and those who educate them in secular schools, will still have to keep the necessary vigilance and attention. Also with college students it would be negligent to let them grow up with scientific, historical and cultural knowledge, without these being balanced with a solid Christian formation: they will not be able to face their challenges if they only retain the catechesis of the sacraments of Christian initiation.

Responsible parents know that guiding them like this takes time, it requires the generosity to think frequently about what their children need, what helps them more and how to communicate it to them and intend to do everything that turns them into "present and active parents", or as one parent proudly claimed to be a "militant father". For this task they are well accompanied by God and count on his grace. So the spiritual life of parents has to do mainly with their home and their children: "it would be a serious mistake if they were to exclude family life from their spiritual development". Sometimes it can happen that, with the enthusiasm for the supernatural and full of good will, some are tempted by extraordinary things that separate them from what God expects of them, for example, being absent from home for several days to make a pilgrimage to a shrine of the Blessed Virgin (even going abroad).

A kidnapped and a Hudson River survivor

A journalist kidnapped in a Latin American country, when he thought he had only a few days left to live, wrote a letter to his wife thanking her for everything she had done for him and apologized for having given more importance to his job as a journalist than his domestic life. "With this remorse I go to my grave". Thank God he was released. I don't know how he took advantage of this new opportunity. What is clear he really appreciated the great value of the family and it is possible that, sometimes, someone will forget this and get absorbed by things that are not the most important.

Something similar is told by a survivor of the famous US Airways flight that in 2009 made a successful emergency water landing in the Hudson River, after its engines were disabled by a flock of birds. When he heard the captain of the plane announce: "Prepare for impact", he reflected as never before, and one of his main conclusions was that, in addition to not wanting to die so young, as from that moment, he wanted to be a better husband and father. He was granted the grace to continue living, and he tells how he was taking advantage of this new life, for example, by not arguing with his wife, and by enjoying seeing his children grow up.

Charity is brotherhood and friendship

The love that Joseph had for his family is also a good incentive to imitate him in our kinship and friendship, to relate to our brothers with the same qualities of his love. And it seems to me that there is no excuse to suppose that for him it was easier because he had Mary and Jesus next to him. The cause of his relationship with them was charity, generous dedication, not expecting anything in return. The same charity that we are expected to practice ourselves, without being governed, for example, by selfishness - usually unconscious - of loving those who treat us well or people we like, but showing harshness or criticism when it is not so. If you love those who love you, what thanks can you expect? Even sinners also love those who love them. And if you lend to those from whom you hope to receive, what thanks can you expect? Even sinners also lend to sinners to get back the same amount (Lk 6:32-34). True charity leads us to loving someone also despite his defects; otherwise it would not be love as Jesus taught us. Indulgence is the attitude that leads us not to increase those deficiencies, but to look for a way to forgive, forget and to find, if that were the case, the best way to correct them.

Consistency and inconsistency in charity

Living charity is the touchstone of true religiosity: Jesus was particularly clear when he said during the Last Supper "that we must love one another as He loved us: by this you will be known as my disciples" (Jn13:35).

This doctrine would seem to be well understood by the policeman who stopped a woman who was extremely angry honking the horn of her car at the vehicle in front of her, and who, in her opinion, had stopped abruptly at the traffic light. After a long while, and releasing this woman, he apologized to her because, he had thought that her car was stolen. When she asked him why had he thought such a thing. The policeman explained to her: Madam, I ordered you to get out of the car while you were furious honking the horn, wanting to drive over the car of that poor old man, cursing, yelling and saying hurtful words. As I watched you, I realized that a rosary was hanging from your rear-view mirror, the car has a sticker on the back that says: "What would Jesus do in my place". Your license plate has a message that says: "Love your neighbor", and another sticker that says: "Follow me to church on Sunday", and also has the Christian emblem of the fish. After seeing all this I assumed that the person who was driving the car could not be the owner of it". The policeman had clear ideas, but this woman did not.

How consistent are we in dealing with our neighbors? What do others think of how we treat them? What do they usually complain about? What specific details can I improve to make those who are by my side happy? Do I love people as they are, without expecting perfections that they don't need to have, as I don't have them either? How do I take care of the life of piety and formation for those people God has entrusted to me?

Chapter 8
Dealings with Jesus, the Savior

You will name him Jesus.
Matthew 1:21

Jesus is the Savior

To both Joseph and Mary were given, with identical words, the task of giving the Child, who would be born the name of Jesus. To Mary it was the archangel Gabriel (Lk 1:31) and to Joseph, an angel appeared in his dreams. The naming ceremony was performed during circumcision. Luke makes a clear statement of how they obeyed: "When the eighth day came and the child was to be circumcised they gave him the name Jesus, the name the angel had given him before his conception" (2:21) and Matthew simply says: "and named him Jesus (1:25).

The name of Jesus is the shortened form of Yehoshua "Yahve saves". Joseph had been given the reason for this name: "because he will save his people from their sins" (Mt 1:21). Jesus is therefore the Savior.

Over time Jesus will say to his apostles, while explaining the parables to them: "Happy are your eyes because they see, your ears because they hear! I tell you solemnly, many prophets and holy men longed to see what you see and never saw it; to hear what you hear, and never heard it" (Mt 13:16). These words could well refer to the humble craftsman of Nazareth who was fortunate enough to accompany Jesus so closely, and together with Mary, contemplate him like no one else. Day by day he would be filled with joy and hope seeing the one who had come from Heaven growing up in order to rescue men from the greatest slavery, which is that of sin.

He never fell into a detached routine when being with the Child. On the contrary, aware of the treasure he had in front of him, he always admired it and let himself be surprised: "Saint Joseph, more than anyone else before or since, learned from Jesus to be alert to recognize God's wonders, to have his mind and heart awake"[54].

It is also an invitation to us, that through faith, we can see and hear Jesus. If we welcome him, the joy of his promises will fall on us: "Happy are those who have not seen and yet believe" (Jn 20:29). We are asked to follow Jesus. And in order to do it with joy and benefit, one needs this attitude of admiration that Joseph had; it is necessary to take an interest in order to understand supernaturally everything that is happening and not stagnate, "to have an open heart and soul" to recognize the wonders of God. May Our Lord help us to pray calmly, to give our prayers the priority they deserve, and not be superficial or get into a routine; not to be inconsistent.

We can approach Jesus, who is "the Way, the Truth and the Life (Jn 14:6), in various ways. Here I would like to highlight the one related to his name: he is our Savior, and this is one of the most important ways of getting closer to Jesus. Of course he is the Master and we have much to learn from Him. Furthermore, he is our friend ("I have called you friends, because everything I heard from my Father I have passed on to you" (Jn 15:15), which will allow us to have profound heart-to-heart confidences. He is also our role model, every virtue that we wish to develop finds its paradigm in him who is "perfectus homo" (perfect man), in addition to being perfect God. But most important all we need is to get closer to the one who forgives our sins, who saves us and redeems us: actions that only Jesus can do because he is the Son of God.

---

54 *In Joseph's workshop*.

Our Lord compares his saving function to that of a doctor. Thus, when he had to reprimand the scribes and pharisees who reproached him for approaching the sinful friends of Levi, recently called to the apostolate, he told them: "It is not those who are well who need the doctor, but the sick. I have not come to call the virtuous, but sinners to repentance" (Lk 5:31-32). "We must have complete faith in the one who saves us, in this divine Doctor who was sent with the express purpose of curing us, and the more serious or hopeless our illness is the stronger our faith has to be" [55]. How much comfort we will obtain when we turn to Jesus knowing the immense good that he can do to our soul, which so often is sinful and imperfect. We will not call on Him from the height of our pride or false security, but from the humility of someone who recognizes to be in need [56], from who requires to be healed.

The privilege of Joseph of contemplating and living with Jesus, the Savior, can be given in some way to each one of us, so as to center and base our lives on Him. The encounter with Jesus is what it takes to be a Christian. Benedict XVI said it with special emphasis: "Being Christian is not the result of an ethical choice or a lofty idea, but the encounter with an event, a person, which gives life a new horizon and a decisive direction" [57]. The invitation is to meet God who loves us, who for our salvation gave up his Son, who invites us to follow Him, and who guides us and gives meanings to all our chores.

Jesus is our way to reach God. Until his Incarnation, what Saint John mentioned was fully carried out: "No one has ever seen God", but with his arrival to this world everything changes, "it is the only Son, who is nearest to the Father's heart, who has made it known." (Jn 1:18). What is offered to us through Him is something very real, not to relate to an abstract "divinity", nor to the God of philosophers (to be the "immovable motor" or the "uncaused cause" means very

55 *Friends of God*, 194.

56 Cf. *Catechism of the Catholic Church*, n. 2559.

57 *Deus Caritas est,* 1.

little to us). We are invited to seek, find and follow the Person of Jesus, God made man: someone who inhabited our land and is still alive; who had a physique and a real face, a specific tone of voice. Or as the Second Vatican Council beautifully says, someone who "worked with human hands, thought with a human mind, acted by human choice and loved with a human heart. Born of the Virgin Mary, He has truly been made one of us, like us in all things except sin"[58]. Someone who awakened love and not a few misgivings wherever He went by.

To know the Gospel is to know Jesus

Leaving aside for a moment the Eucharist, the sacrament that allows us to join to the same Jesus that Saint Joseph cared for, another unequivocal way to find ourselves and learn to follow Jesus Christ is that of the Holy Scriptures, particularly the Gospels, as long as we read them with an ecclesiastical sense, namely according to the authentic interpretation that the Church has given them. To know the Gospels is knowing Jesus. I suggest you read attentively the following reflection: "When you open the Holy Gospel, think that what is written there - the words and deeds of Christ - is something that you should not only know, but live. Everything, every point that is told there, has been gathered, detail by detail, for you to make it come alive in the individual circumstances of your life".

"God has called us Catholics to follow him closely. In that holy Writing you will find the Life of Jesus, but you should also find your own life.

"You too, like the Apostle, will learn to ask, full of love. "Lord what would you have me do?..." And in your soul you will hear the conclusive answer. "The Will of God!" Take up

58 *Gaudium et spes*, 22.

the Gospel every day, then, and read it and live it as a definite rule. This is what the saints have done"[59].

This is a good way to reach the promised holiness: to confront our whole life with that of Jesus. ("What do you want me to do?" "What would you do in my place?"), begging for his grace in each conversion. To watch Jesus praying we see how we could pray better every day. Watching the hidden world of his life it becomes clearer to us that the important thing about our task is not so much the recognition by others, but to love God and others while doing so. And thus we can continue with the different alternatives of our life: dealing with others, the attitude towards what is harder or the false accusations, the relationship with material things, etc.

"Whoever sees me, sees you"

In Jesus Christ we find the "human face of God and the divine face of man"[60]: both a close-by God and the model of what we are called to be through our vocation to holiness. Is our frequent reading of the Gospel characterized by being that of someone who wants to discover something central in his life every time? "Saint Joseph, who never got tired of contemplating and caring for our Savior, by reading the Gospels gets us the grace of feeling challenged to imitate Jesus, and that we have the hope with his help be able to achieve it"

I once heard a priest tell about a girl who prayed a bold but very accurate prayer. "Lord whoever sees me, sees you". This should be the case for every Christian, because by taking his Baptism seriously, he must fully identify himself with Christ and reflect him wherever he moves. We have already quoted those words of Pope Francis about how Jesus saw the tenderness of God in Joseph's fatherhood. Something

59 *Forge*, 754.

60 John Paul II, *Ecclesia in America*, 249.

similar is asked of each one of us; parents are called to be like an icon of God's love for his children; the priest must embody the mercy of the One whom he represents sacramentally; he must thus serve everyone, but especially sinners, the sick and the needy. Each baptized person must reflect to his friends that way of being of Jesus who knows how to keep company: as when he cried for Lazarus, or came to the rescue of his discouraged disciples who were going back to Emmaus, or when he showed Simon Peter that he still trusted him.

One might imagine that that quality of "showing Christ" is an almost impossible task; the ideal is too high and personal deficiencies plentiful. More so if one takes into account that it is primarily a matter of identifying oneself with Him, of being Christ himself [61]. But discouragement is obliterated when we remember that "for God nothing is impossible" (Lk 1:37; Jr 32:27), and that it is not something that occurred to us recklessly but that it is an ideal to which we have been called by Jesus Christ himself (cf. Jn 15:16). Therefore, we can enjoy the same assurance as Saint Paul, who affirmed that he was "quite certain that the One who began this good work in you will see that is finished when the day of Jesus Christ comes" (Phil 1:6).

"Only with you can I be better"

A young architect said that he proposed to his girlfriend saying, "I want to be with you, because only with you can I be better". He was inspired by a phrase from a movie, but he had made it his because after experiencing many disorders, he has also experienced that the relationship with his girlfriend inspired him to conquer himself, and in her he found the hope of improving. Altering what is necessary, many times we can say this to Our Lord.

---

61 It is a frequent teaching in Saint Josemaria: "But we must join him by faith, letting his life manifest itself in us, so that it can be said that each Christian is no longer "alter Christus, but ipse Christus", Christ himself! (*Christ is passing by*, 104).

As we get closer to the Most Holy Humanity of Jesus Christ, Our Lord is gradually 'formed' in us (cf. Gal 4:19) and he is transforming us, making us better. We can experience it, first of all when receiving the sacraments, and also in the different forms of prayer: meditation, the prayerful reading of the Gospel, the Holy Rosary and the Stations of the Cross. If no obstacles are placed to sanctifying grace, what happens progressively is what the Apostle says: "I live now not with my own life, but with the life of Christ who lives in me" (Gal 2:20). The Christian will be transformed, and he will do things that he previously could not even imagine. How is it possible that I have had that courage to witness to God if normally I had been shy and reserved? How has it happened that I was usually mercenary and selfish and am now helping without expecting anything in return? Christ makes us be so.

When they asked Cardinal Joseph Ratzinger's secretary what impressed him most about the Cardinal, after thinking about it he replied: "the respect in his voice when he pronounces the name of Jesus"[62]. If this man of God acted like this, so much more Joseph. May God help us to spread that devotion so that we can get closer to the only one who can save us.

62 Peter Seewald, *Benedicto XVI, Una vida*. Ediciones Mensajero, p. 542.

CHAPTER 9
LIVING FOR GOD

They took him to Jerusalem to present him to the Lord.
Luke 2:22

JOSEPH TAKES THE CHILD TO THE TEMPLE

Forty days after the birth of Jesus, when the time established by the law of Moses was fulfilled, his parents went to the Temple of Jerusalem to comply with the double prescription of the purification of the mother (cf. Lev 12:2-8) and the presentation and rescue of the firstborn son (cf. Ex 13:2.12-13). Legal obligations that in a strict sense did not apply to them but they also wanted to fulfill: Mary was always very pure and had nothing to "purify", and Jesus, God made man, did not have to be "rescued".

We can deduce the role of Joseph in this episode. He would go along with Mary, who was carrying the Child in her arms. "At the gates of the Temple, he bought two turtledoves for the offering, since he lacked the resources to buy a lamb. Thus, the humble couple remained framed in the group of the poor and, therefore, no one noticed them when they crossed the esplanade"[63].

He complied with the legal prescriptions with a religious spirit, and saw in it an opportunity to offer to the Father that Child who had come into this world to rescue all men, since we are all affected by original sin. When presenting him with devotion, without being a priest, "Joseph was the first to offer God a 'holy and perfect sacrifice', the Word Incarnate in the

63 *Joseph's silence,* p. 104.

womb of Mary, his wife, and never before has the world seen anything so valuable offered to God. It seems as if God had arranged things so that the last Patriarch would once again exercise the quasi-priestly functions that were exercised…by the old patriarchs"[64].

But, shortly after entering, there was someone who did become aware of what was happening: "Now in Jerusalem there was a man named Simeon. He was an upright and devout man: he looked forward to Israel's comforting, and the Holy Spirit rested on him. It had been revealed to him by the Holy Spirit that he would not see death until he had set eyes on the Christ of the Lord. Prompted by the Spirit he came to the Temple: and when the parents brought in the child Jesus, to do for him what the Law required, he took him into his arms and blessed God" (Lk:2 25-28). It was the Holy Spirit that prompted him to recognize in that creature, the son of poor parents who did not attract attention, the Messiah and Savior, not only of the Jews but of everyone. This supernatural discovery filled him with joy and led him to exclaim: "Now, Master, you can let your servant go in peace, just as you promised: because my eyes have seen the salvation, which you have prepared for all the nations to see: a light to enlighten the pagans and the glory of your people Israel" (Lk 2:29-32).

Faced with this unexpected welcome, "the child's father and mother stood there wondering at the things that were being said about him" (Lk 2:33). From the evangelical messages it was clear that Jesus was going to be the Savior of the Jews (cf. Mt1:21), but now this salvation was extended to all people.

The Holy Patriarch would take advantage of this pilgrimage to renew his devotion and dedication to the service of God. With much joy and gratitude he would say 'yes' again, he was willing and delighted to do what he asked of him, that it did not matter the sorrows he had had and those he would have in the future, and specially, he would ask him

---

64 *Joseph, Mary's husband*, pp 134-135.

for the grace to be able to fulfill with much affection his task of protecting the Child and his Mother. Mary would act in a similar way: once more she would pronounce her "fiat", her "let it be", making herself available again, which in addition, in a surprising and unexpected way, would be expanded with the prophecy that the old Simeon pronounced at that time: "a sword will pierce your own soul" (Lk 2:35). Although both spouses did not understand the meaning of what they were hearing, they did realize that God was asking them for a sacrificial love. And since what affected Mary affected Joseph, he also accepted whatever it could mean.

The first commandment: love God above all things.

This mystery of Our Lord's life invites us to direct our lives to the One to whom we belong. "Know that the Lord is God: that he made us and we are his, his people and the sheep of his flock" (Ps 99:3). If Jesus wanted to be "presented" before the Lord God, how much more should we recognize our dependence on him, knowing that we owe him what we are and what we do. It is part of the task of loving God above all things, of living the first commandment: "You must love the Lord your God with all your heart and with all your soul and with all your mind" (Mt 22:37).

Faced with such a divine "demand", we could misinterpret it as if God were in need of us, jealous of his rights and prerogatives, demanding a kind of unconditional surrender with the intention of overwhelming us. But, far from it, whoever created us out of love and for us to be happy, points out this commandment to us precisely as the way to reach our fullness. The starting point is that "God is love" (Jn 4:8) and that "He loved us first" (Jn 4:19).

The first divine commandment, like the others, is not arbitrary or conventional: it is wise and the most convenient to our nature. Perhaps what is meant is better understood if we relate it to other precepts, for example: "You shall not kill", "You shall not steal" or "You shall not lie". What would happen if God said something like: "I abolish these commandments, it will not be a sin if they do the opposite: you can kill, steal, lie and I will not be offended", No! It would be our destruction, human coexistence would be unfeasible, we would not achieve happiness. For the same reason - that we participate in his eternal bliss - God established that we love him. This is what Saint Augustine recognizes with his classic cry from the bottom of his soul: "You made us Lord for yourself, and our heart is restless until it rests in you" [65]. For this reason, "God's first call and just demand is that man accept him and worship him" [66]. On a regular basis, but especially on retreat days, it helps a lot to reflect on how oriented we are towards God, what priority we give him, how surrendered to him and to his will we live. And something similar tries to do the pious soul in every moment of prayer by saying: "I am yours, I was born for you, Lord, whatever you want from me..." [67].

A SPECIFIC WAY OF LIVING FOR GOD: THE HOLY MASS

The surrender to God is shown in specific day-to-day things: seeking to know the Word of God and making it work in what concerns us; accepting lovingly the alternatives of family life, of work, by accepting its costs (illness, poverty, etc.). We can renew this living for God in various way - for example, by offering our daily work or in a personal prayer - but there is one way that stands out, the Holy Mass.

The Mass, which is the Eucharist considered as sacrifice, is such a sublime mystery that it is "the source and summit of the Christian life" [68]. As we know, it was instituted by our Savior on the eve of his death on the Cross, precisely to perpetuate for centuries that sacrifice of his body and his

---

65 *Confessions*, 1,1.

66 *Catechism of the Catholic Church*, n. 2084.

67 Words inspired by what Saint Josemaria said that on of his grandmother prayed.

68 *Catechism of the Catholic Church*, n. 1324.

blood. He thus left the church the memorial of his death and resurrection[69]. The graces that we can obtain from each Mass are immeasurable. Undoubtedly that depends on divine generosity, but also on our personal dispositions (faith, love, humility, etc.).

Following the command of Christ, "Do this in memory of me", the Church once again renews the Lord's offering at each mass. He does it through ministers ordained for that purpose (the presbyters), and the laity, by virtue of the real priesthood granted in Baptism, can join in their own way by offering to God the Father the best sacrifice: his beloved Son which is renewed in each Eucharist.

For this reason, everyone must always be active, and I am not referring now to aspects such as singing, reading or passing the collection plate, but rather to what the Catechism of the Catholic Church recalls: "In the Eucharist the sacrifice of Christ is also the sacrifice of his members", drawing useful consequences from his truth: "the lives of the faithful, their praise, sufferings, prayer and work are united with those of Christ and with his total offering, and so acquire a new value"[70]. Hence, the mass, is not only something that happens between Jesus and the priest who is at the altar: but each one can and must get involved, especially joining what one has to offer to the holocaust of Jesus. Saint Josemaria, a priest who loved the Eucharist and who taught many how to participate in it, liked to say: "our Mass, Jesus". Hopefully we will consider it that way.

69 Cf. id, n. 1323. "The memorial is not only the memory of the events of the past, but the proclamation of the wonders that God has done for men (cf. Ex 13:3). In the liturgical celebration these events are made. In a certain way, present and current (Id. n. 1363).

70 N. 1368.

An office clerk kissing his desk

I remember the father of a family who worked in an office and had learned to consider the Mass as the center and root of his life, and to seek the sanctification of all he did through his union with the sacrifice of the altar. Besides going to mass every day, he had the habit of kissing his desk when he arrived at his work and when he left it: as he was protected from prying eyes, he repeated to himself that that was his "mass" and that was the "altar" for him. It was a real application of what he had heard: "All the works of men are done like at an altar, and each one of you, in that union of contemplative souls that is your daily work, says in some way his mass, lasting twenty-four hours, awaiting the next mass, which will last another twenty-four hours, and so on until the end of our lives" [71].

To live Holy Mass lovingly is something of such an entity that it requires our preparation in order to avoid distractions or to fall into a habit. That preparation includes: arriving on time, updating the faith in this mystery, perhaps reviewing the readings or even, for those who can, praying for a while.

But a most remote preparation is also necessary, which implies for example, reading periodically about this sacrament, either one of the many good books available or the part that deals with it in the Catechism, and it also entails getting more doctrinal formation by studying a treatise or attending some theology classes.

When we participate devoutly in the mass, we learn to live the logic of the Eucharist, that is to surrender: to join ourselves to Jesus who accepts us lovingly. His way of acting is "catching" on us, and thus we learn how to give ourselves to others. For a father or mother, this will not be an inspiration to go on a mission to another country or continent, but to continue working on their own character, expanding their capacity for service or empathy, to put a little more order into

71 St. Josemaria, Notes for a meditation, 19.III.68, quoted by Burkhart-Lopez. *Vida cotidiana y santidad en la enseñanza de San Josemaria*, 1.3.2.2.

their life, to know how to find time for their family, and for so many people with whom they relate and who are somehow waiting for some spiritual help.

OFFERING ONE'S LIFE WITH ITS LIGHTS AND SHADOWS

We offer our entire real life, it will resemble that of the Holy Patriarch: "Saint Joseph's life is a good example of this: it was simple, ordinary and normal, made up of years of the same work, of days - just one day after another - which were monotonous from a human point of view"[72]. The real life that we want to offer to God is also made up of our weaknesses, just as Joseph being most holy, had to show God at that time his imperfection, the pain, of not having something more adequate for the birth of Jesus. The words of the Pope in his exhortation on Saint Joseph are encouraging when he explains that: "The history of salvation is worked out "in hope against hope" (Rom 4:18), through our weaknesses. All too often, we think that God works only through our better parts, yet most of his plans are realized in and despite our frailty"[73]. Let us frequently renew the desire to surrender to God who we are and what we have, without expecting idyllic situations of perfection, success or excellent mental conditions.

How good it would be to be able to have in each Eucharist the same affection that Joseph showed caring for Jesus and offering him that day in the Temple. Once again we can go to him through the pious prayer that is offered to prepare for mass, first with a declaration of what his life was: "O blessed Joseph, happy man whose privilege it was, not only to see and hear that God whom many a king had longed to see yet saw not, longed to hear, yet heard not: but also to carry him in your arms and kiss him, to clothe him and watch over him!", and then ask God the Father that just like Saint Joseph "was found worthy to hold in his arms and with all

---

72 *In Joseph's workshop*

73 *Patris Corde*, 2.

reverence to carry your only-begotten Son, born of the Virgin Mary, enable us this day to receive worthily the sacred Body and Blood of your Son".

Chapter 10
Joseph's grandeur in his humility

And entering the house, they saw the child with Mary, his mother and kneeling down worshiped him.
Matthew 2:11

Joseph is not mentioned at the adoration of the Magi

Some Magi arrived in Jerusalem from far away and with amazing simplicity asked: "Where is the infant king of the Jews! Because we saw his star as it rose and have come to do him homage" (Mt 2:2). As we contemplate them, we might be moved to consider the Epiphany of Jesus from its main meaning: making himself known to the Gentiles. We could also meditate on the exemplary attitude of faith of these magi, which would not be out of keeping with the praise to the faith of the ancient patriarchs in the Epistle to the Hebrews. Of them it could well be said: "by faith they followed the star, left their land and safety; by faith they recognized the Messiah in a poor child and worshiped him; by faith they offered him their gifts".

But now I suggest to the reader to approach the episode of Jesus from the specific point of view of Joseph. Without a doubt, seeing that such remarkable characters had come from afar to worship the Child would fill him with admiration once again. He had already learned that living according to God is a constant adventure. He would be especially pleased by the recognition these Gentiles made of Jesus.

However, a detail that draws the attention to Matthew's report is that Joseph is not mentioned at all. It is very likely to think that he was present. He would not leave the Virgin alone with the child Jesus; and if at the time the magi arrived he had been out working, he would have returned at once, because if the presence of such a retinue did not go unnoticed to the inhabitants of Bethlehem, it would be less so to him. In fact, after a few hours he is mentioned when events precipitate and it was necessary to flee from there. But in this account it was not necessary to mention him: the important fact was to show what happened with those magi and the Child, who, of course, was with his mother.

Faced with such a fact, many would probably feel disappointed not to appear, or to have them play a seemingly unimpressive role. This was not Joseph's attitude. "To the humble and holy life of Joseph God added - if I may put it this way - the lives of the Virgin Mary and of Jesus, our Lord. God does not allow himself to be outdone in generosity. Joseph could make his own the words of Mary, his wife: *Quia fecit mihi magna qui potens est,* the Mighty One has done great things for me, *Quia respexit humillitatem*, for he has looked upon his handmaid's lowliness"[74].

Joseph was aware of the place he should occupy. His nobility allowed him to be a docile instrument to perform whatever God asked of him. The same nobility that he showed when the shepherds appeared on Christmas night and about which Federico Suarez has this to say: "From the obscurity of being in the background, without being noticed, he takes as natural and appropriate the adoration of the Child, the deferences to the Mother and the fact that little or no attention was paid to him. Herein lies not a small part of his grandeur: he never expects anything for himself. But then, when the time comes to give, there he will be occupying the first place. In responsibility and in work, in effort and in duty, he is never a spectator, but a main character"[75].

And with regard to the presentation of the Child in the Temple, the same author will say something that is perfectly

74 *In Joseph's workshop.*

75 *Joseph, Mary's husband*, p. 113.

applicable to the style that characterized his entire life: "It does not seem that....it would matter much to him to play this role which seems like being secondary, or any other, if that's what he is supposed to do, as long as it was what God wanted from him. This attitude, customary to him, being in silence, contemplating from a discreet half-light what concerns the Son and the Mother, is also profitably instructive to us, if we know how to apply it to our life. This humble man never did anything to attract attention to himself (which is something that we cannot say, at least most of us), nor did he care whether posterity would know about him or not. Attentive to his work, he had no time for narcissism. His humility freed him from that kind of leprosy that sometimes attacks men..., as far as distorting them: attachment to one's work or reputation"[76].

The need of humility

With this attitude of self-forgetfulness, our saint teaches us an important part of the humility we need to live because our limited condition demands it, especially in relation to God. Ultimately it is about imitating the virtue that Jesus lived from his birth in a manger till his humiliating death on the Cross. The same humbleness that reflects a God who annihilates himself by becoming man (cf. Flp 2:6-11) and who will have more than enough moral authority to say to us "learn from me for I am gentle and humble in heart" (Mt 11:29).

By Joseph's behavior, we understand that humility is not mere submission or withdrawal; it is compatible with developing a great personality. Only with quietness and passiveness he could not have solved the challenging tasks that he had to face. "The Gospels give us a picture of Joseph as a remarkably sound man who was in no way frightened or shy of life. On the contrary, he faced up to problems,

76 *Joseph, Mary's husband*, pp. 138-139.

dealt with difficult situations and showed responsibility and initiative in whatever he was asked to do".

The way to open up to God and to others

Humbleness is the way to open us up to God: "God resists the arrogant and gives his grace to the humble" warns both Peter (1 Pet 5:5) and James (Jas 4:5). When we are arrogant we lose our position in front of God, and we relate to him in a way that we shut ourselves off from his grace: it is as if we said "I am self-sufficient", "I have the right to ask God...", or we dare judge him: "what He does seems wrong to me". On the other hand, if we truly recognize our dependence of God, his superiority in intelligence and generosity, it will be easier for us not to credit to ourselves what is not ours. "What do you have that was not given to you?" And if it was given, how can you boast as though it were not? (1 Cor 4:7). We will thus be in a position to invoke his grace, ("God, be merciful to me, a sinner", cf. Lk 18:13), and the Lord, who always wants our good, will gladly grant us what is more convenient to us.

Pride, the vice opposed to humility, is like a many-headed monster, it has many manifestations. In moments of reflections such as retreat days, it is extremely useful to examine how we are living humility and to see what aspects of our behavior need to be rectified. And not just during a retreat. It is very helpful to discuss this virtue with our Lord in personal prayer. For example, it may help to meditate slowly on point 263 of *Furrow*, as it raises some twenty obvious signs of lack of humility.

As long as someone strives to improve in humility, one needs not be discouraged if one notices the persistence of bad inclinations or one's resistance to change. What happens is similar, *mutatis mutandis*, to what happens with the lawn in a garden. It is always growing, and at times it threatens to turn the land into a wild jungle; but if you cut it regularly, you get a wonderful garden. If we keep our arrogance at bay through the struggle, cutting off shoots such as the desire to be noticed, to want to give a good image or to have the last word, our life will have a certain beauty. It will be a question of rectifying the intention, of repenting, of asking for forgiveness -also from the people we may have influenced- of going to confession, of starting and restarting.

Perhaps the inclinations of pride will never be completely uprooted. Just as the method to have a beautiful garden is not to uproot all the vegetation or kill it with herbicides, since there may be nothing left, neither the method to humbly develop the talents received is to systematically hide them, or not to aspire to improve or to wish for a fair recognition. It is more about pruning, of channeling the exuberant vegetation of the garden of our existence, seeking to give glory to God, rectifying the intention and serving others. Thus progressively the Christian is gaining and meanwhile sanctifying himself.

With humbleness comes joy. Joseph daily contemplated his Holy Wife and the Child, and he served them unconditionally. His spirit rejoiced deeply with the immense fortune that had been bestowed upon him. He was not disturbed by what others might think of him, nor was he distracted by comparing himself to anyone. How was he not going to be happy being next to God made man? How was he not going to enjoy sharing the day with the most holy and good woman in all of history? He was extremely grateful and forgot all about himself.

A fair forgetting oneself he is a source of humbleness and of joy, and the opposite, of sadness. "Most of the conflicts arising in the interior life of many people are products of their own imagination: 'the things people have said, what they are thinking, whether I am appreciated…'. The poor soul suffers, through his pathetic foolishness, harboring suspicions that are unfounded. In this miserable mood everything makes him bitter and he tries to upset others also. All this because he doesn't wish to be humble, because he hasn't learned to forget himself in order to give himself generously in the service of others for the love of God" [77]. In order to achieve this personal detachment, the solution is not so much to refuse to think about oneself - since some of it is necessary- as to frequently ask oneself what others need from me.

Two ways to advance in humility

One could say that there are two ways to achieve this virtue. One is by humiliations. Failures, defeats or disgrace will prune in various ways the excessive desire for excellence. Whoever thought himself capable of anything, and therefore superior to others, discovers that he is like others: he also has his limitations, powerlessness and mistakes. It happened to Saint Peter and the other apostles who learned this science through their own sins. The student who fails an exam for which he had studied has the same opportunity, or the worker who is not given the promotion he hoped for, or to the mother and wife of the previous cases, who suffers for her son and her husband. According to Saint Bernadette "many humiliations are needed to obtain a little humility"

The other way is called by Jacques Philippe "the experience of God" [78], it has to do with experiencing the divine greatness and one's personal poverty. It is no longer the reflections that one can have from one's own limitation, but the action of grace that shows, crystal clear, the divine goodness before which human virtue turns pale. "Meeting with the living God destroys all pride; by knowing God in his power, his majesty, man understands that he is nothing, that he is nothing before God". Joseph experienced it by seeing the humility of God, who annihilates himself by incarnating and becoming a Child whom he has to take care and protect. All other things considered, each of us can acquire something of this virtue as we seek to unite ourselves with our Lord: when we adore the Eucharist, when we kneel to

77 *Friends of God*, 101.

78 Cf. J.Philippe, *La Felicidad donde no se espera*, Rialp, Cap. 13.

accuse ourselves of our sins and implore his forgiveness, when we confidently and serenely accept God's plans which we do not always understand.

The empty cart

Alfonso Aguiló relates a story with a moral. "I was walking with my father when, coming to a bend, he stopped and after a short silence asked me: Apart from the singing of the birds, do you hear anything else? I sharpened my ears and answered: I am hearing the noise of a cart. That's it, said my father, it is an empty cart. I asked my father: How do you know that it is an empty cart, if we still cannot see it? Then my father replied: It is very easy to know when a cart is empty for its noise. The emptier the cart, the more noise it makes. I became an adult and now, when I see a person talking too much, interrupting everyone's conversation, being inappropriate or violent, showing off with what he has, being arrogant or thinking he is better than others, I have the impression of hearing the voice of my father saying: "The emptier the cart, the more noise it makes" Humility consists in silencing our virtues and allowing others to discover them. "No one is emptier than the one who is full of himself" [79].

How different from the arrogant is the path that Joseph shows us! His life was truly full. He is the holiest of all creatures with original sin. He lived an incredible existence alongside the Incarnate Holiness and the "full of grace". Angels communicated with him. He had very many virtues. And that is why he was discreet, he knew how to keep his place, he did not brag, he did not seek to be a protagonist or to make a noise. Won't I have something to rectify, to look more like Saint Joseph?

79 Interrogantes.net.

Whoever struggles to be humble will be like our saint: a suitable instrument for what our Lord wants to work in him and with him. And consequently, he will live happily

Chapter 11
Supernatural sense of events

Get up and escape into Egypt until I tell you.
Matthew 2:13

A joy that did not last long

The joy for the visit of the Magi did not last long. That very night, using the usual system, an angel communicated to Joseph in peremptory terms: "Get up, take the child and his mother with you, and escape into Egypt and stay there until I tell you, because Herod intends to search for the child to do away with him" (Mt 2:13). There is no need of much imagination to realize the drama of the situation.

There wasn't much to think about or time to waste. He trusts what he is told and sets off. "Joseph got up and, taking the child and his mother with him, left that night for Egypt" (Mt 12:14). They left with what they were wearing and little else. Among the few things they carried was the gold that the Magi had providentially offered the Child, and some tools that would allow them to sustain themselves at their final destination. The trip was especially hard, mainly because of the fear of being caught. It was not just anybody who wanted to kill the child, he was no other than the king, a particularly cruel and unscrupulous man. There were several days of anguish and fatigue. Probably Joseph had chosen the longest route for reasons of prudence: the shortest and most traveled would be better guarded.

Once they started, and in the silence of the night, he would reflect on what was happening. Thinking with human logic, the matter sounded crazy and even contradictory. But, as Saint John Crysostom points out and Saint Josemaria comments, this was not his reaction: «"On hearing this, Joseph was not shocked nor did he say: This is strange. You yourself made it known not long ago that he would save his people, and now you are incapable even of saving him - we have to flee, to set out on a long journey and spend a long while in a strange place: that contradicts your promise. Joseph does not think in this way, for he is a man who trusts God. Nor does he ask when he will return, even though the angel left it so vague: Stay there, until I tell you to return. Joseph does not object: he obeys and believes and joyfully accepts all the trials". Joseph's faith does not falter, he obeys quickly and to the letter. To understand this lesson better, we should remember that Joseph's faith is active, that his docility is not a passive submission to the course of events. For the Christian's faith has nothing whatever to do with conformity, inertia or lack of initiative»[80].

"He stayed there until Herod was dead. This was to fulfill what the Lord had spoken through the prophet: I called my son out of Egypt" (Mt 2:15). Joseph was God's instrument to facilitate the fulfillment of the prophecies about Jesus, who would give rise to the new People of God. It had been foreshadowed by Moses, who as a child was providentially saved from dying under Pharaoh's orders and then saved his people from oppression by leading them out of Egypt. "Christ's whole life was lived under the sign of persecution. His own share it with him (cf. Jn 15:20). Jesus' departure from Egypt recalls the Exodus and presents him as the definite liberator of God's people"[81]. It is likely that the Nazareth carpenter did not fully realize what this meant but, once again, he trusted God and listened to him, thus preparing the salvation of so many.

80 *In Joseph's workshop.*

81 *Catechism of the Catholic Church*, n. 530.

When we don't understand God's doings

Things happen in our life that confuse us and may seem meaningless to us. Joseph's serene attitude helps us to learn "God's method", the divine logic, sometimes so different from ours, but always so full of meaning, even if we cannot understand it: "For my thoughts are not your thoughts, my ways not your ways - it is the Lord who speaks. The heavens are as high above the earth, as my ways are above your ways, my thoughts above your thoughts" (Is 55:8-9). Joseph has a supernatural vision made up of a gigantic faith in God and his work, accompanied by a confident hope and unconditional love.

As a result of this usual attitude of the Holy Patriarch, Pope Francis says: "Often in life, things happen whose meaning we do not understand. Our first reaction is frequently one of disappointment and rebellion. Joseph set aside his own ideas in order to accept the course of events and, mysterious as they seemed, to embrace them, take responsibility for them and make them part of his own history. Unless we are reconciled with our own history, we will be unable to take a single step forward, for we will always remain hostage to our expectations and the disappointments that follow" [82].

It is true that God wants our happiness and for this he has created us, but is also true that happiness does not consist in carrying out our projects, and much less our whims. God knows more than we do. He has the whole picture in his "head". And he knows that sometimes it is more convenient for us to lose, and then to win. In those moments when the

---

82 *Patris Corde*, 4. Also in this document he confesses that he recites this prayer daily, that has served him in times of uncertainty or difficulty: "Every day, for more than forty years, after Lauds, I recite a prayer to Saint Joseph taken from a book of French devotions of the 19th century, of the Congregation of the Religious of Jesus and Mary, which expresses devotion, trust and certain challenge to Saint Joseph. "Glorious Patriarch Saint Joseph, whose power knows how to make impossible things possible, come to my aid in these moments of anguish and difficulty. He takes under your protection such serious and difficult situations that he entrusted to you, so that they have a good solution. My beloved Father, all my trust is in you. Let it not be said that I have invoked you in vain and, as you can do everything with Jesus and Mary, show me that your goodness is as great as your power. Amen" (id.2).

work of God puzzles us, the invitation is to meditate on the "story of our personal salvation", on what God has done for each of us. I was told of a woman who in moments of difficulty reasoned in this way before the Lord: "Until now you have always helped and accompanied me. Usually, you have given me much more and better things than what I had dreamed of. I am sure that now, although I do not understand it, you will also arrange things for my benefit and my family's".

When we notice that God asks us to trust him, it may help us to realize that he trusted us first. Just as we find encouragement to love our Lord, in the fact that: "God loved us first" (1Jn 4:19), in the same way it helps us to know that He trusted us first. It is enough to think that he grants us freedom with all his potentiality: we can come out a winner or a loser, we can be obedient and good children, or go astray. He could say to each married person: "I entrust you with your spouse, I entrust these children to you. Do you think it is a small task? Take care of them for me". Something similar happens with every vocation: God runs the risk of calling someone. Are we not then to trust Him even though we do not fully understand him. Hopefully we may deserve the praise of the psalmist: "Lord of Hosts, blessed is the man who trusts You" (Ps 84:13).

Where was God?

In the presence of certain tragedies, it is relatively common to hear or read statements from afflicted and bewildered people who question, "And where was God?", we can even be one of those who asks. For example, we may have experienced it during these years of pandemic. Where was God? Why did he allow it? The answer will have to be sought personally, but in general terms it could be said that God guided us to grow inwardly, to develop virtues, to re-think our work and relationship with others and with things. Of course, there were sorrows, losses, and powerlessness, but they were not in vain.

In those years, and whenever there is a difficulty, it's as if God would say: "Here I give you this tribulation so that, making it yield like a treasure, you may receive the prize that I have prepared for you", "I am counting on you to soothe the pain of those who are by your side", "I rely on you, so that through this test you may collaborate with me in the work of Redemption", "With this difficulty I offer you a happiness that you did not expect", "I have in mind to regale you through this problem with a growth in humbleness and in detachment of unnecessary burdens" [83].

The supernatural vision of faith, hope and charity will lead us to discover God behind everything: whether joyful or painful. And in both cases, doing what He knows how to do: to love. Thus, if there is trust in God, we will always see the good side of things, we will experience that what Saint Paul said is true: "We know that all things work together for the good of those who love God" (Rom 8:28).

A reflection of Benedict XVI may be of use to us: he tells us of his "failure" to pass a thesis for qualifying to be a professor of theology and saw his work rejected. He admitted that the trials of those difficult years had a healing effect. His verbatim words are worth it, despite the fact that they refer to a specific type of activity: "I had obtained the doctorate very fast. If I had qualified with the same ease, I would have had an excessive awareness of my ability: my self-esteem would have been too one-sided. And so, at one time, I was completely diminished. That does you good: to have to acknowledge all your neediness again, not to appear as a great hero, but as a humble candidate to be a professor who is on the edge of the abyss and must get used to doing what you need to do. In a sense I absolutely needed a humiliation, and this came to me for a good reason….I believe that for a young man it is dangerous to achieve one goal after another with ease and receive praise from all quarters. Then it is good to stumble over your limits. To be treated critically sometime. To have to go through a negative phase, to recognize your

83 *Omnia in bonum.* p. 13.

limits. That you may not just go from triumph to triumph, but may also suffer defeats. That is needed by every person in order to learn to value oneself correctly, to have stamina and, not least, in order to think with others. And just that will help him not to judge hastily and from above, but to accept another view in a positive way, even in his tribulation, in his weaknesses" [84].

"Stay there until I tell you": the uncertainty

Part of the test of Egypt included the uncertainty about the future: "stay there until I tell you" (Mt 2:13). How long would it be? Weeks, months, years? No data; just wait to be told.

How must Joseph have reacted to that question? "Of course the provisional state to which he was forced by circumstances was as uncomfortable as it could be for anyone else, but this discomfort did not affect him as deeply as could have affected others. He was a simple man with a simple job, so he did not have in his thoughts grandiose plans or definitive works to which he 'consecrated' his life, the kind of works that are made thinking of posterity" [85]. Joseph was able to patiently face this test because he knew how to combine decision with detachment. He took seriously what he had been assigned which was the only reality: he had to find a lodging, find the means to survive, interact with the neighbors... On the other hand, he was willing to return whenever the angel would tell him.

The fact that he was in a provisional state or realizing that the circumstances were far from ideal, were not an obstacle for taking care of his task in a holy manner, seeking the best possible conditions and giving his best response. "Joseph was not the sort of person who never starts something for

---

84 Peter Seewald, *Benedicto XVI, A life,* pp. 322-323.

85 *Joseph, Mary's husband*, p. 160.

fear of not finishing it. He did his work, in Egypt the same as in Nazareth, day after day, one hour after another, and he did not stop to think if he would not be able to finish the work he had started in case he had to change places or simply in case he had to die" [86].

In our life we also have uncertainties from time to time. Due to an illness, a transfer, a situation of unemployment. Imitating the attitude of Saint Joseph in Egypt will lead us to realize we must do what is within our power, of living the present, day by day, being attentive to the breath of the Holy Spirit. Thus we may move away from useless worries to problems that have not yet shown up, and which may never occur. To sanctify the duties of each moment the advice is clear: "Do your duty 'now', without looking back on 'yesterday', which has already passed, or worrying about 'tomorrow', which may never come for you" [87].

How rich is the outlook of the things that God offers us. It surpasses our capacity: however great it may be, it turns pale by its immensity. Even if things get difficult, even if we do not understand them, even if it seems to us that the ideal conditions are not present, just like Joseph let's activate the "supernatural mode", let's try to look with God's eyes through faith, hope and charity. And with this patience we will possess our soul (cf. Lk 21:19); whatever happens we will always have peace and serenity.

86 Id. p. 161.

87 *The way*, 253.

Chapter 12
The true fear: rejection of sin

He was afraid to go there.
Matthew 2:22

The return from Egypt

After an unforeseen period of time for Joseph and unknown to the rest, he again received supernatural indications, in this case to return to his country. "After Herod's death, an angel of the Lord appeared in a dream to Joseph in Egypt, and said: Get up, take the child and his mother and go back to the land of Israel, for those who wanted to kill the child are dead" (Mt 2:19).

It must have been a source of great joy shared with Mary. We do not know the reaction of the Child, among other things because we don't know his age at that moment. Although they must have settled down among the people and in the place where they lived and they may have had some regret about leaving them, the will to fulfill the divine commandment and return to their homeland prevailed. Without further delay "he got up, and taking the child and his mother with him, went back to the land of Israel" (Mt 2:21).

Upon arriving in his land, he learned that Archelaus, son of the cruel Herod, ruled in Judea. Matthew tells us then that he "was afraid to go there" (Mt 2:22), his mission in life was to protect Jesus, and he has his senses well sharpened for this task. Saint Josemaria commented on this event: "In the different circumstances of his life, Saint Joseph never refuses to think, never neglects his responsibilities. On the contrary, he puts his human experience at the service of faith. When he returns from Egypt, "learning that Archelaus had succeeded his father Herod, as ruler of Judea, he was afraid to go there." In other words, he had learned to work within the divine plan. And to confirm that he was doing the right thing, Joseph received an instruction to return to Galilee"[88]. His fear was not cowardice but real prudence. It is not a virtue but recklessness to ignore real and avoidable dangers, and Joseph did not want to take unnecessary risks for his family.

Alerted again in dreams, "he left for the region of Galilee. There he settled in a town called Nazareth. In this way the words spoken through Prophets were to be fulfilled: "He will be called a Nazarene" (Mt 2:22-23).

Caring for the Child, Caring for Grace

Before Joseph's vigilant prudence, "we should always consider whether we ourselves are protecting Jesus and Mary, for they are also mysteriously entrusted to our own responsibility, care and safekeeping"[89]. It can be said that this Child is given to us, who wants to live and grow in the life of each one of us (cf. Is 9:5; Lk 2:52). Are we defending the grace that has been entrusted to us? The first thing we should agree to protect is, as they say, "being in God's grace". "There is nothing better in the world than to be in the grace of God"[90]. For this we need a gift of the Holy Spirit, not always well understood: the gift of fear of God. It does not mean to be afraid of him who is our Father, but to be aware of his greatness and majesty, it is the fear, the grief, of offending him.

Just as Joseph took care with all his qualities and strength of him who had been entrusted to him, and arranged so that nothing would harm him (he fled from Herod, he did not want to come near Archelaus), every responsible Christian

88 *In Joseph's workshop.*

89 *Patris Corde*, 5.

90 *The Way*, 286.

wants to arrange things so that nothing harms his union and friendship with God, in order to avoid sin [91]. There are things that "kill" the Child that has been entrusted to us. We can't flirt with such a sad possibility. We have to know how to flee, know how to be afraid of going "there", to those places where what is important would run risks. Everyone must know himself. Today, many must be careful with the handling of their devices, which can put them instantly in situations that they may regret later. And you will always have to take care of your own home, your spiritual formation, your apostolic mission.

One must avoid above all mortal sin, but also venial sins, especially deliberate ones, those that we accept even knowing that they are an offense to God and harm to us. Dishonesty at work, isolation that leads to omissions in charity, exaggerations or distorting reality when speaking, judging and criticizing without charity and without justice, and a lot of other possibilities (of thought, word, deed and omission), of which it is convenient to examine oneself.

Sometime after arriving in Nazareth, when the Child was twelve years old, the Holy Family went up to Jerusalem. There Jesus stayed in the Temple without his parents' knowledge, for supernatural reasons, which at least initially they did not understand (cf. Lk 2:41-50). Mary and Joseph were always diligent in taking care of him, but a boy his age had a certain autonomy in the sense that they should not always be on top of him; he was the one who decided to stay. They were not responsible for the loss of the Child. But, it hurts to say, sometimes we are responsible for the loss of him, for the estrangement from him due to our negligent behavior, of little affection. How good it is to recognize our mistakes and sins, and to know how to ask forgiveness for them.

---

91 *The Way*, 386: "Do not forget son, that for you on earth there is only one evil, which you will have to fear, and avoid with divine grace: sin".

DID JOSEPH HAVE SINS?

Of the members of the Holy Family, Joseph is the closest to us insofar as he is the only one who shares original sin with us. No sin emerges from his conduct as described in the Gospel. His initial deep doubts cannot be considered faults. He was looking for the best way to act according to God's will. Hence when he secretly thought of abandoning Mary, it is made clear to us that he did so because he was being fair. With the data that he had and following his delicate and well- formed conscience, he reached such resolution - heroic by the way - but which was not necessary to put into practice because God had other plans. Rather his attitude resembles his dear wife, who certainly had no sin, but to whom "did not spare her pain, exhaustion in her work, or trials of her faith"[92].

Joseph may have had sins, but there is no point in guessing about them. More sense and benefit is to think of ours. Not to torture ourselves or to sink into sadness, but to get to know ourselves, repent, and avoid them in the future.

IMMERSE OURSELVES IN THE DIVINE MERCY

I don't think the most important part of a retreat is "knowing how to cry over our sins", as a troubled woman said, who questioned by a friend of hers, admitted that she had not succeeded. I believe that in days of retreat, the most important thing is to grow in the awareness of the love and trust that God has for us. It does not mean that by the desire to correspond to the divine goodness hatred of our guilt may break out. Rarely will we be granted to "cry" over them, but may God wish that our repentance may have the firm determination to avoid them. Hence, making a good confession is more congruent with a well-done retreat: not so much for its length but for its repentance.

92 *Christ is passing by*, 172.

It is possible that in a retreat it is convenient to make preferably once in a while, a general confession, covering all the previous sins which we can remember. But in these cases, and always, we must abandon ourselves to the mercy of God, he throws our sins into the ocean of his mercy (cf. Mic 7:19). The past, is over. God is greater than our sins.

This attitude of confident abandonment will lead us to avoid the perfectionism of seeking to feel well by trying to do everything right. It is a utopia. By definition we are imperfect and sinners. Our anticipation and our commitment must be to love God and allow us to be loved by Him. Of course we wish to do things right and avoid sin, but definitely we will not achieve it while we are in this world. So, it is very important to learn to live with our limitations, fighting over and over again to overcome them, but knowing that God loves us this way. This attitude must be extended to dealing with others, and thus knowing how to live with the weakness of others; it will always be present, and it must be assumed, loving and accepting people as they are will help them to improve.

THE FIGHT AGAINST THOSE WHO HURT US

The gift of the fear of God also helps to convince us that sin is never a gain, it is always a loss. It is bad business to exchange our friendship with God for the little trinkets that different sins offer us. It was clear to Thomas More when he was talking to his wife Alice at the Tower of London. She wanted to persuade him to swear as the king requested and thus save his head. Whoever was a good Catholic and at the same time a good citizen could not with a clear conscience agree to the unjust wish of the king. "If I swear, how much longer do you think I can live?", "About twenty years", "and do you want me for twenty years to lose eternal life?"

If when reviewing your own life, as usually happens on retreat days, bad habits are discovered, it is time to turn more decisively to God's grace to uproot them. It is not a reason for discouragement to discover that you have a bad character, or have an addiction, or that you often live for yourself without helping others, or that there is a lot of disorder with time and things, or that you don't take God much into account, or whatever... It is time to decide or renew the intention of going to confession often, of speaking in the spiritual direction of these struggles, and of seeking mortifications "synchronized" with these needs, for example: to smile more despite fatigue or little desire to do so, or to start and finish work on time.

How regular am I in my confessions? Are they contrite and concrete? Do I go about it simply and sincerely, knowing that I am going to "accuse myself" and not "excuse myself"?

In any case, a Christian knows that the main objective cannot be limited to not sinning, but to accept the invitation to do very good things: imitate Jesus, make many people happy, and seek holiness.

Just as God told Joseph: "Son of David, do not be afraid!" (Mt 1:20), so he seems to tell us: "Do not be afraid!" We need to set aside all anger and disappointment, and to embrace the way things are, even when they do not turn out as we wish. Not with mere resignation but with hope and courage. In this way, we become open to a deeper meaning. Our lives can be miraculously reborn if we find the courage to live them in accordance with the Gospel. It does not matter if everything seems to have gone wrong or some things can no longer be fixed. God can make flowers spring up from stony ground. Even if our heart condemns us. "God is greater than our hearts and he knows everything" (1 Jn 3:20)[93].

With the courage and abundance of graces God gives us we dare continue accepting his calls, continue converting ourselves. We should only be afraid of what drives us away from God and his plans; on the contrary, let us not be afraid, like Joseph, of receiving Mary and Jesus in our lives. Every moment of prayer and even more so, every spiritual retreat can be real opportunities to welcome the graces offered us from Heaven.

93 *Patris Corde*, 4.

Chapter 13
Sanctify work and daily life

And he went to live in Nazareth.
Matthew 2:23

He dedicated himself to work

"And being warned in a dream he left for the region of Galilee. There he settled in a town called Nazareth" (Mt 2:22-23). After living in Bethlehem and in exile in Egypt, Joseph returned with his family to his hometown. Thanks to the joy of the reunion with loved people and places, it was easier to start over. He had little money, since he had forcibly emigrated without prior planning, as do those who move from a city or country to an offer of a better job. And after the period of their absence, many things had changed. It was necessary to recover or find a new house, and get back to work, perhaps initially with few tools because with the relocations he must have lost a few. He was poor but at the same time he was "rich" because he continued to have the treasures of Jesus and Mary by his side.

And what did he do in Nazareth? The usual, he dedicated himself to his family and to work, sanctifying ordinary life. "Joseph was, we have said, a craftsman from Galilee, just one man among many. What had life to offer to someone from a forgotten village like Nazareth? Nothing but work: work every day with the same constant effort. And at the end of the day, a poor little house in which to rest and regain energy for the next day" [94]. A simple and sacrificed work, but with a unique reward: because in that poor and small house he shared

94 *In Joseph's workshop.*

living with God-made-man, and with his Blessed Mother, who was his wife. That would be a little piece of heaven on earth. They would live for each other, forgetting themselves but focused on the other, pendent with love on what God was doing: the Redemption of the human race.

In time, Jesus would be recognized by the work of his father: "Is this not the son of the craftsman?" (Mat 13:55). They knew Joseph because of his work, because of his trade. As we know so many people, not always knowing their name: the supermarket cashier; the florist; our doctor or dentist; the car mechanic; the man at the garage where we keep the car; the hairdresser; the maths teacher, etc.

It is very useful to meditate that the most holy man sanctified himself by working on ordinary things. He didn't have to do spectacular things or be ahead of his time. For example, he had no need to develop a chain of carpentry shops spread throughout Galilee, nor to be an internationally renowned furniture designer. Perhaps, if he had lived in our century, God would have expected something else from a craftsman like him, because he would like him to incorporate advances in technology or marketing. But then it was not necessary, and if he was so common, what did his great holiness consist of? In the love that he expressed.

Work and love

Federico Suarez describes his love at work saying: "His work was not comfortable or brilliant, but thanks to it that small family got ahead; it was monotonous, without great prospects, without masterpieces, but his perseverance did not decline, nor did his patient and daily effort. He was not restless, always displeased with his task, constantly changing from one task to another, permanently dissatisfied and seeking in the change of occupation a tranquility that was impossible to find outside of himself, because when one does not love his work, it is impossible to find any kind of satisfaction, no matter how many times you change tasks".[95]

We can imagine Joseph as being punctual in delivering his work. From time to time he would be forced to pick up the pace a bit if the deadline for a delivery approached. He would finish the work well, taking care of the details or the conclusion of things by dint of correcting whatever hadn't gone well. This would be reflected in the quality of his tables and chairs, which would not wobble or unglue easily. The founder of Opus Dei, who was a forerunner in the task of spreading the search for holiness through work said that the Holy Patriarch was not the man of easy miraculous solutions, but a man of perseverance, effort and, when needed ingenuity. And to illustrate this, he compares the story related in an apocryphal gospel that tells how one day the parts of a bed came out uneven to Joseph, and the Boy would have performed the miracle of stretching the shorter rod, with which Joseph was extremely happy. Neither Joseph, nor Jesus would act like that. Miracles are reserved for other occasions. Not a cure for incompetence nor an easy way to dodge effort.[96]

If things went well for Joseph and if he was esteemed by others, it was because he was "a worker performing his job in the service of his fellow citizens, who has a manual ability obtained through years of effort and sweat"[97]. The sanctity of his working life, recognized by the Church with the feast of Saint Joseph the Worker every May 1st is explained by his love for the Lord and for others.

A Christian will imitate him if it can be said of his task that he achieves that ideal so wisely mentioned: "Work is born of love, it is a manifestation of love, and is directed toward love"[98]. If the cause of what you do is not pride, the desire to assert yourself, or to feel well: but to love God and the

95 *Joseph, Mary's husband,* pp. 207-228.

96 Cf. *In Joseph's workshop.*

97 *Ibidem.*

98 *Ibidem.*

recipients of each task: students, diners, clients, patients or whoever. If the task is done in such a way that it reflects the affection of the person who took care of details for love, if the ultimate purpose of their work is to give glory to God and not for vanity or the desire for recognition.

God expects from us the offering of work done in such a way that it is pleasing to him. He expects us to sanctify ourselves in this way. Who by divine vocation is in the middle of the world cannot spend much time in the temple. If possible, it is very clear that it is convenient to go to pray in churches, oratories or chapels. Moreover, on days of retreat, it may be convenient to spend long periods in an oratory or a hermitage, even most of the time. But this would not be convenient for the day to day: God, through others and society, expects to find us in our workplace.

And when referring to work, all everyday circumstances are included. Not only the great work of the house, which corresponds to all the inhabitants in one way or another. Work is also the illness or the limitations of age: accepting care with patience, depending on others, the exercises to be done, drinking water when we are not thirsty but are told it is necessary, accepting the limitations of movements or forgetfulness with good humor. And it is also work, to look for work when you are unemployed.

On one occasion I was giving a talk to school girls about the sanctification of daily work. I was trying to illustrate that doctrine which teaches that for work to be pleasing to our Lord it needs to be well done and out of love, within reasonable possibilities. I don't remember what practical examples I gave, but I do remember that the teacher of the students, who had stayed to listen, interrupted me saying: «That's the same thing my husband tells me! When I tell him, I don't know how to cook, he replies: "Put affection into it"». That is our objective when working for God, doing it with affection. I suppose that in the case of that teacher, young and newly married, it would consist not only in putting good will but in consulting a You Tube tutorial, or a recipe book, or the traditional resource of asking your mother.

A SMALL PLAN AND A THREADED NEEDLE

Doing work with love, imitating Joseph -and also Mary and Jesus, who thus sanctified the years of their existence- implies taking care of the small things, having fineness, discovering the needs of others. In negative terms, it is expressed in this judgement: "By neglecting small details you could work on and on without rest and yet live the life of a perfect idler" [99]. Those who systematically arrive late or delay the return home while staying at work would incur in these faults. He who does not stop to program his activities well, and for that reason runs from one place to another, always out of breath and, in the best of cases, apologizing for his non compliances. He who does not know how to deal with the different alerts and notifications on his cellphone, interrupting unnecessarily the attention of what he is doing even looking superficially at the received messages, thus making frequent mistakes.

By contrast, I remember two simple examples which at the time moved and helped me see when someone does things lovingly. Both happened at the 2013 World Youth Day in Rio de Janeiro. When taking the bus that would take me from the airport to my accommodation, I asked the lady who sold the tickets on the bus, at which stop I had to get off to go to a specific address. She simply replied that she would let me know. Some time and several kilometers later she made a signal for me to get off, and when doing so, to my amazement she handed me a little drawing, which she had made on a blank sheet, showing the route I had to take from the stop to the precise address I was going. That was truly a "Carioca" [100]welcome! and an example of work done thinking of others.

A few days later, a button came off my jacket. I asked the other priest with whom I shared accommodation if any had a needle and black thread. One of them told me: "I do, my

99 *Furrow*, 494.

100 Nickname used to mention the people who lives in Rio de Janeiro.

sister gave me a sewing kit for this trip". Great was my surprise when I opened it and noticed that the needle was already threaded with black thread: only a sister who considers the needs of her brother or his companions, could think of such a detail so appreciated by an inexperienced hand!

Spirit of service

In order for the task to be carried out to be holy, "it should have a feature which was basic to Saint Joseph's work and should be so for every Christian: the spirit of service, the desire to contribute to the well-being of other people. Joseph's work was not self-centered, even though his active life made him a strong and forceful personality. When he worked, he was aware that he was carrying out God's will; he was thinking of his people, of Jesus and Mary, and of everyone in Nazareth" [101].

This is well exemplified in a paragraph by Henri-Michel Gasnier: "The inhabitants of Nazareth would frequently request his services: when a door would not close, when the leg of a bench broke, when a shelf was rotten, when some newlyweds were setting up their home, what the Pharaoh said referring to his prime minister was repeated: "Go and see Joseph"" [102]. And a few lines from the homily "In Joseph's workshop" complements this idea of service. "I am sure Joseph knew how to lend a hand in many difficulties, with work well done. His skilled work was in the service of others, to brighten the lives of other families in the town; and with a smile, a friendly word, a passing quip, he would restore confidence and happiness to those in danger of losing them".

His attitude of service would lead him not infrequently to lend a hand to the neighbor who required his help. And he would have no problem, for example, in being a courier

101 *In Joseph's workshop.*

102 *Saint Joseph's silences*, Palabra, 1980, p.82.

when he traveled, carrying a message or a small package to be delivered to a relative who lived elsewhere. He would dedicate time to a sick person in his town in need of care.

And I, why do I work? What am I looking for with that work to which I dedicate so much time? Am I aware of having talents or abilities that I have to put at the service of the common good? Do I have the sensitivity and generosity to realize when someone who needs my service cannot repay me adequately? Those who work with me, can they easily count on my collaboration, or do they find that frequently "I only do my things"?

If God expects us to sanctify at work, in the broad sense already expressed, it is reasonable that a large part of the resolutions made in moments of prayer, or in a retreat, should point in the direction of improving it and of doing it with more charity. Perhaps it means reviewing schedules, and thinking of small mortifications that contribute to a job well done. Rectifying the intention and being more aware of your work partners and of those you serve. With Saint Joseph it will be easier to specify those desires of improvement.

Chapter 14
When the pain shows up

See how worried your father and I have been looking for you.
Luke 2:48

Jesus voluntarily remains in the Temple

After narrating the return of the Holy Family from Egypt and their settling in Nazareth, a prolonged silence about their lives begins in the Gospels. The only data we have is that "the child grew to maturity and he was filled with wisdom, and God's favor was with him (Lk 2:40). Years of a normal existence for Joseph and family, our Redemption is taking place in that atmosphere of normality, work, learning and family life.

But the serenity and calm of these years was disturbed by an unexpected event. It was on the occasion of what we contemplate in the fifth joyful mystery of the Holy Rosary: the child Jesus lost and found in the Temple. "Every year his parents used to go to Jerusalem for the Passover feast. When he was twelve years old, they went up to the feast as usual. When they were on their way home after the feast, the boy Jesus stayed behind in Jerusalem without his parents knowing it. They assumed he was with the caravan, and it was only after a day's journey that they went to look for him among their relations and acquaintances. When they failed to find him, they went back to Jerusalem looking for him everywhere" (Lk 2:41-55).

For his parents this was a cause of great sorrow. Despite the usual care of the one who was a faithful custodian, the Child stayed away from his parents, who suffered unspeakably. It is understood that they did not find him until a few days later, because at that age Jesus could go back in the caravan either with the women or with the men. Mary presumed that he was going with Joseph and Joseph that he was going with Mary. When they regrouped for the night, they realized his painful absence, and they retraced the road and only "three days they later they found him in the Temple, sitting among the doctors, listening to them and asking them questions" (Lk 2:46).

His parents could not know that at such moment their son was acting in order to teach us the priority of God and his things. "Jesus did not want Mary and Joseph to suffer, but to teach men of all times a lesson even though it was painful to his parents" [103].

When they found him, "they were astonished" (cf. Lk 2:48). What a capacity for astonishment for those who, despite having lived with him for twelve years, did not cease to be surprised: they had always contemplated him and had tried to discover the richness of his life. This amazement may have been due to the ease with which he handled himself. "since all those who heard him were astonished at his wisdom and his responses" (Lk 2:47). But perhaps, along with astonishment, they were perplexed to see that, apparently, the Child was not concerned about his parents' worry.

They had been for three days in a state of mind that Mary herself would describe thus: «And his mother said to him: "My child, why have you done this to us? See how worried your father and I have been"» (Lk 2:48). "Worried" is the word that expresses the feeling they both had. The two holiest creatures had anguish: tension, dismay, fright, and everything that this strong word means. The Child's answer apparently did not clarify things much, at least not at that moment. "Why were you looking for me? Did you not know that I must be busy with my Father's affairs?" This is what the evangelist Lucas adds: "But they did not understand what

---

103 Pedro Beteta, *Descubriendo a San José en el Evangelio*, Cuadernos Palabra, Cap. 10.

he meant". Even with their great holiness, neither Mary nor Joseph understood at that moment what he wanted to say to them" [104].

They did not understand him: but it seems that they had no big problem about it. "They were humble and they did not mind not understanding Jesus's answer; like children, it was enough for them to know that there was an answer, even when they did not know what it meant. They knew there was a reason even if they did not penetrate it. It was enough, for them [105]. About Mary this is added: "And his mother kept all these things in her heart". The Virgin Mary meditated on these events, ruminated on them, she made them the object of her conversation with God, and it is to be presumed that, based on praying, she would eventually have understood them. And Joseph would have done the same, also benefiting from what his Holy Wife meditated on in her heart and shared with him.

Joseph learned by praying, by considering things in the presence of God and from this perspective he learned to integrate in his life the various difficulties that arose. "St Joseph's life was simple, but it was not easy" [106]. In previous pages it has been related how he overcame the anguish over Mary's pregnancy, how he accommodated poverty in his life and how he faced the flight into Egypt. It was also considered when he heard old Simeon prophesy that the Virgin Mary would have to be associated with the Cross of her Son - although different words were used - and he understood that he would have to go along that path in some way. A path that was going to be very happy, but not exempt from the sacrifice that love often demands.

One of the devotions with which the faithful have honored St. Joseph over the years is to contemplate his sorrows and joys. There are various traditions to describe

---

104 *Omnia in Bonum*, p. 106.

105 *Joseph, Mary's husband*, p. 236.

106 *In Joseph's workshop.*

them. Some of them have to do with the so-called "seven Sundays of St Joseph": in preparation for his feast on March 19, on each of the previous Sundays, a sorrow is proposed later complemented with a joy. This contrast of sorrows and joys is expressed by a verse of the motet "*Te Joseph celebrent*": *Tu natum Dominus stringis, ad exteras Aegypty profugum tu sequeris plagas: amissum Solymis quaeris, et invenis, miscens gaudia fletibus*. "You embrace the newly born Lord; you follow him in his flight to the foreign lands of Egypt; when lost, you look for him in Jerusalem, and you find him, mixing thus joys with tears". The same as in our life, sorrow is not the last word: after the Cross comes the Resurrection.

Sorrow alongside our walking

We all come across sorrow at different times in life. It is unavoidable. To live is to face difficulties. What can we learn from the Holy Patriarch in those moments? "Even through Joseph's fears, God's will, his history and his plan were at work. Joseph, then, teaches us that faith in God includes believing that he can work even through our fears, our frailties, and our weaknesses. He also teaches us that amid the tempests of life, we must never be afraid to let the Lord steer our course. At times, we want to be in complete control, yet God always sees the bigger picture" [107].

To pray, to trust, to use the means available and to focus on what is important: Jesus and Mary. God, who is faithful, never failed him. Yes, there were times when things got very difficult. But in his fidelity, composed of the theological virtues and of great humility, he did not allow himself to doubt God or his providence. It was his turn to take heed when he received concrete clues on how to move forward, to use the means available to improve the present and continue to keep a watchful eye on his treasures: Mary and Jesus.

---

107 *Patris corde*, 2.

To follow Jesus Christ is also to be willing to carry the cross (cf. Mt 16:24). But accepting that pain does not mean having to enjoy it as if it were an end in itself: it is sacrificial love. In short, it is forgetting ourselves to open up to God and to others. And as a consequence of this generous love -"until it hurts" as Teresa of Calcutta says- joy comes. It is good for us to follow the advice of The Way: "I want you to be happy on earth. And you will not be happy if you don't lose that fear of suffering. For, as long as we are 'wayfarers' it is precisely in suffering that our happiness lies" [108].

In order to advance with benefit on "the subject of pain" it will be necessary to propose particular things, such as not complaining about the frequent daily setbacks, seeing in them an opportunity for growth or purification, or to collaborate on the salvation of souls. Regarding the daily setbacks, there is always something to choose from: the weather, the mood of others and the mood with which one gets up after a night in which one has not had enough rest; the volume of traffic, the delays imposed by others and by the circumstances, the amount of work, etc.

It is also beneficial to look positively for mortification, especially when it helps us in the fulfillment of our duties. What would be a better proposition? Not to put jam on your toast or to make an effort to get to work on time? Each one will decide. Perhaps avoiding sweet things would enrich our will and serves to be more demanding with ourselves in administering our time, but it is also possible that in order to look after a delicate health jam is of great importance. The inner struggles must be "synchronized" with what God expects of each person in the loving fulfillment of his obligations. Someone who got information by reading the newspapers proposed the following mortification: First prayer, then the newspapers, thus "forcing" himself to give priority to his morning encounter with God.

---

108 N. 217

Pain is not always understood

Holiness is not something that depends mainly on what each one is doing. It means mostly to let God act in our lives. Therefore, one needs humility in the presence of Providence. There will necessarily be events that we will not understand, that exceed our ability to comprehend. It would make no sense to rebel, to demand answers from God. There are things that are only revealed to the "small and humble", like Joseph and Mary, and are hidden from the powerful" (cf. Mt 11:25), that is to say, the arrogant, the self-sufficient and the insufferably conceited. Although Mary and Joseph did not understand everything right away, with their humble fidelity, they were able to face situations serenely.

I was surprised by the way a grandmother taught her grand-daughter from a young age to cope with pain and difficulties. She spoke to her, like so many other pious people to their children and grandchildren, of the importance of offering to God the things that are hard to accept, of giving them to Him as one who makes an offering: a fatigue, an act of obedience or a convenient service, even when she did not feel like it. And she suggested to say at every opportunity: "For your love, Jesus!". But her originality was in the motivation when she said "For your love, Jesus!", it is as if she were depositing a small silver coin in heaven, and thus at the end of her life she could find a treasure. Naivety, some might say, but just in case, it is better not to forget the words of Jesus: "Truly I tell you: if you do not convert and become like children, you will not enter the Kingdom of Heaven" (Mt 18.3).

The Holy Patriarch, the man of a simple life but not exempt from sorrows and difficulties, can intercede for us when we go through similar circumstances, and with his eloquent silence will help us to trust God when we do not understand what is happening.

Chapter 15
The value of obedience

He was subject to them.
Luke 2:51

He preceded him, paying attention

The event of the Child Jesus in the Temple is finished by the Evangelist Luke saying: "He then went down with them and came to Nazareth and lived under their authority" (Lk 2:51). Upon returning to his town, he went back to what had been the norm until then: obeying Mary and Joseph, paying attention to them. The God-made-man respected family authority, he wanted to let himself be told what to do by two creatures, that not matter how holy they were, they were still creatures. He continued to live, according to his age and circumstances, under such authority. He was carrying out the plan of Redemption that meant obedience, as opposed to Adam's rebellion, and that would lead to giving his life as our ransom. "As by one man's disobedience many were made sinners, so by one man's obedience many will be made righteous" (Rom 5:19); he "was humbler yet, even to accepting death, death on a cross" (Phil 2:8).

Jesus' obedience was preceded by that of his parents. Mary, always attentive to God, accepted without hesitation what the archangel Gabriel proposed to her. Joseph will follow the same path of acceptance of the divine plans. Every time that in his dreams God ordered him something, he immediately obeyed him: to take Mary as his wife; to name the child Jesus, to flee to Egypt; to return to a specified region of Israel. Also, with his example he would teach the Child this virtue, that is why Pope Francis will call him: "father in obedience". "Saint Luke is especially concerned to tell us that Jesus's parents observed all the prescriptions of the Law: the rites of the circumcision of Jesus, the purification of Mary after childbirth, the offering of the firstborn to God (cf. 2: 21-24). In every situation, Joseph declared his own "fiat", like those of Mary at the Annunciation and Jesus in the Garden of Gethsemane. In his role as the head of the family, Joseph taught Jesus to be obedient to his parents, (cf. Lk 2:51) in accordance with God's command (cf. Ex 20:12)[109].

In Joseph's obedience, his fidelity is shown, full of faith and humility. This attitude magnifies him, since "he kept the commandments of God without wavering, even though the meaning of those commandments was sometime obscure or their relation to the rest of the divine plan hidden from him"[110]. His mature personality is perfectly compatible with his openness to divine plans. And it is precisely this openness that makes him great. It allows him to reach much higher and further than what his vision and experience would indicate. And because of this he becomes "God's trusted man".

Obedience to God and to the Church

Obedience is a positive virtue and more necessary than what one may think. It is not an evil necessity to ensure for instance the cohesion of the institutions. It is not something reserved to children who have to practice it in order to safeguard their integrity and to mature. Not unique to the Religious: vows of poverty, chastity and obedience are familiar to us. This virtue helps us all, because it is the path that invites us to contrast the judgment of others to our own, which -let us be sincere about it- is often so poor.

The one we have to pay attention to first is God. It is logical that it should be so. He is the one who knows and loves us the most. Although the example is not perfect, it can help

---

109 *Patris Corde*, 3.

110 *In Joseph's workshop.*

us to understand this virtue by comparing it with the users' manual of different devices. Regarding a mobile phone, for example, we are told how to turn it on, how to charge the battery, the things that optimize its use and those that would spoil it. We find guidelines on internet connections, the use of the camera and the alarm clock, and a multitude of apps that it already has or that can be installed. And we trust the indications they give us. They come from the manufacturer and are for their perfect use. How much more should we know and accept the indications of our Creator! He knows very well what we need, what makes us grow, what leads us to happiness. We win when we fulfill God's commandments, and not only those that we like the most or that can be kept with relative ease: everyone helps us, we need them all.

Obeying God is, on the other hand, the path to holiness, a sure way to please him. Other things in themselves would not unite us so much to Him. "Obedience is worth more than sacrifice and docility, more than the fat of rams (1 Sm 15:22) "God does not need our work, but our obedience" [111]. We would love that God the Father could be as happy with us as he was with Jesus, Mary and Joseph. Obedience is the path. "Anybody who receives my commandments and keeps them, will be one who loves me. And anybody who loves me will be loved by my Father, and I shall love him and show myself to him" (Jn 14:21).

To achieve salvation, Jesus also wants us to obey his Church, which was established on this virtue. "Anyone who listens to you, listens to me; and anyone who rejects you, rejects me" (Lk 10:16). This is the extension of the saving action of Jesus. There we find Jesus himself. He is in the sacraments, in the Word of God, in the teachings of his authentic magisterium. Sometimes we will find very clear lights. Other times, things can be more complex. But trust and faith must be the same. We cannot be selective. "I agree with the Church when it opposes the death penalty, but not with what it says about contraception and 'in vitro'

111 San Juan Crisostomo, *Matthaeum Hom*. 56.

fertilization. It is not a club or a political party to which we adhere by its statutes or platform, while reserving the right to reform them. Our adherence is supernatural. We are not asked a blind obedience, in the sense that our ability to reason is annulled, on the contrary, we are encouraged to understand and deepen our knowledge. But, in any case, we have to be willing to obey, to humble our intelligence until, God willing, we understand: sometimes it may be on this earth, and in some cases we may have to wait. This is Joseph's teaching included in that gospel line: "But they did not understand what he told them" (Lk 2:50). When it is difficult for us to accept some indication, perhaps it is time to remember that warning: "If obedience does not give you peace, it is because you are proud" [112].

Nobody is unaware of the fact that the obstacle to this virtue is not only our distrust or pride. Sometimes it can be the limitations of the person in charge, even in the Church, which is both divine and human. The Lord, "often speaks to us through other people. But when we see their defects or doubt whether they are well informed -whether they have grasped all the aspects of the problem- we feel inclined to disobey" [113]. But if we look at things from a supernatural standpoint, if we see things with the eyes of faith, we will know how to distinguish a limitation, which does not invalidate the will of God, from our pride and its resistance to accept what is asked.

Another subtle problem arises when we judge in the Church while having insufficient data. It can happen that pious people, informed by the press or by other media, fall into the recklessness of judging the actions or words of the Pope or a bishop. It is impossible to judge accurately the magisterium and the activity of the Roman Pontiff just by what the newspaper headlines say. It is naïve and unjust. Beyond the simplistic deformations of this type of communication, not only do we not have the data, but it will not usually be

112 *The Way*, 620.

113 *Christ is passing by*, 17.

our competence. "Do not judge and you will not be judged" (Lk 6:37). Someone may love the Church very much, but his love cannot go beyond "sentencing" what this or that ecclesiastical authority does well or less well. Great part of his love for the Church, and for those who represent it, will consist in increasing the sense of responsibility for their own holiness, and praying for them. There may be exceptions to what has been said, which will require great prudence and humility to build communion and not to hinder it.

Obedience in everyday life

Frequently this virtue will show in being open to the opinion of others. Naturally each human being is limited, and God uses the relationship with others to overcome those limits. How much others have to teach us!, how much we can learn! One problem may be obstinacy: "Only the stupid are obstinate: the very stupid are very obstinate" [114]. A person can spoil his life, or at least impoverish it, by persisting in his ideas: we are not talking about giving up our convictions, nor "letting someone else handle us". But just as the one who "prescribes his own medicine" and ignores the prudent doctor can end badly, or not finish his cure, a person may lose the possibility of growing, maturing, or progressing in virtues, if he does not accept the advice, the guidance given to him by people who love him well.

A name for obedience is "docility". Docile, from the Latin "docilis" is the one who learns easily. It is often of great benefit to have spiritual accompaniment, or spiritual guidance -which was the centuries-old term. We go further and with less difficulties if we have the prudence to be accompanied by those who know the way and the obstacles, by those who look at us with the objectivity we lack in personal matters. "No one is a good judge in his own cause". It is a grace of God to have help of this kind: something to be thankful for and not

114 *Furrow*, 274.

to get badly accustomed to. It is received with advantage if you have the humble attitude of wanting to learn, of making yourself known as you really are, without the absurd desire to come out well. Docility will lead you to trust the advice given, without it taking away your personal responsibility. A good spiritual director will rarely tell you exactly what to do; he will usually open horizons, suggest points of struggle, encourage you at a time of trial, and help each one to discern in prayer what God is asking of him at different times of his life.

I have met people who for years have prayed to find a good spiritual guide: what a good request to make if they have not yet found him.

The desire to continue growing through adequate formation is also a sign of docility. On the path to holiness, there is so much to learn! And above all, so much to put into practice! We need a lot of knowledge: about our faith, about the world, about ourselves, about the spiritual life, etc. And not for the sake of erudition, but for "transformation": learning new things, and frequently reviewing things already known, looking for how to live them in our ever more dynamic life. In this sense, formation will never be considered finished.

Someone might wonder: obedience at home? Yes, of course, and not only by children to their parents. Also by husband and wife who must obey each other in their different fields. Without a competitive spirit, always in search of a common goal, which is to love each other and carry out that shared project that is the family. "Give way to one another in obedience to Christ" (Eph 5:21) is St. Paul's advice to spouses.

Another field of this virtue is at work. There are mainly organizational and disciplinary reasons for living it. But a Christian is not limited only to those reasons to pay attention. He knows how to transcend them and finds in obedience something higher. He freely wants to imitate his Master. That is why, when he obeys, he also learns to overcome the rebellion of disorderly self-love, and to adequately bear the inevitable imperfections of his bosses.

If Jesus obeyed, it was because his parents "ordered him". Whoever has the duty to command, has a way of obeying God's plans who counts on specific people to give orders in the family, at work, in society, and in the Church. It would be comfortable, and very dangerous, to ignore the task of leading others when he has such an assignment. But it will be necessary to lead with a will to serve hence, with temperance and rectitude. Remembering that it is a task of service, that whoever has a responsibility of this type is not more or better than others and much less is a position of personal privilege. Benedict XVI recalled in a quotation from Origen how the Holy Patriarch commands: "Joseph understands that Jesus was superior to him while he was submissive, and knowing the superiority of his minor, Joseph commanded him with fear and restraint. Let everyone reflect: often a person of lesser value is placed above people better than him, and sometimes it happens that the one who is inferior is worth more than the one who seems to rule over him. When someone who has been elevated in dignity understands this, he will no longer be puffed up with pride at his higher rank, but will know that his inferior can be better than him, just as Jesus was subject to Joseph" (Homily on St. Luke, XX, 5, SC p. 287)[115].

Whoever prays with St. Joseph may wonder: How is my docility? Do I let myself be said things I dislike or do I reject them? Am I stubborn? Do I systematically reject the orientations of those who love me well? When it is my turn to command, do I do it with a desire to serve, with refinement and humility? God wants us to understand that "he who obeys grows". Joseph amplified his life by letting himself be guided by God's plans: his life reached unsuspected horizons. If he had refused, insisting on his plans and projects, he would have missed the treasures that thanks to his docility he deserved.

115 *Celebración de las Vísperas*, 18.III.2009.

Chapter 16
Joseph's death

Very well, good and faithful servant...
enter into the joy of your Lord.
Matthew 25:21

Maintaining the usual discretion that the Scriptures have kept regarding Joseph, nothing is mentioned in them about a certain fact: the death of the Holy Patriarch. As to the moment when it happened, we can only guess. For example, there is a tendency to think that at the beginning of Jesus' public ministry, he no longer lived, since he was never mentioned. Thus, when the episode of the wedding at Cana is told, only the presence of his Mother and the disciples is mentioned; presumably, if this party had been celebrated while Joseph was alive, he would certainly have been invited and mentioned.

The few references we have of him in this period seem to suggest that, if he had died, it would not have been long before, as they continue to remember him. Thus, when Philip talks to Nathanael about his great discovery, he tells him: "We have found the one Moses wrote about in the Law, the one about whom the Prophets wrote: he is Jesus son of Joseph, from Nazareth" (Jn 1:45). And Jesus' countrymen also keep Joseph in mind and are astonished to see Jesus and hear him, and when he just returned to Nazareth after having preached and performed miracles in other places, they wonder: "Where did the man get this wisdom and these miraculous powers?" and they ask themselves "This is the carpenter's son, surely?" (Mt 13: 54-55).

It seems reasonable to assume that he died surrounded by the love and attention that Mary and Jesus would give him. This is what that prayer asking for the grace of a good death says: "May I die like the glorious St. Joseph, accompanied by Jesus and Mary, pronouncing those sweet names which I hope to bless for all eternity". The Holy Virgin would show her immense affection taking care of him. She would console him, help him to pray and to enliven his hope. And Jesus, love-made-man, how many details of affection would he have for him who had cared so much for him and loved him!

Mary and Jesus suffered grievously when Joseph died. They had a very lively faith and hope, but that did not stop them from suffering. They knew that he was beginning to enjoy a great prize, but they missed him. How often they would remember him in their conversations. We can entrust ourselves to Mary and Jesus when we have to suffer the experience of going through mourning for the loss of a loved one: they will help us to cope with those painful moments of uncertain duration with peace, remembering with gratitude everything we have experienced, and they will obtain for us the hope of a reunion at the end of our life.

Joseph left this world when the doors of Paradise, that his adopted Son would open, were not yet definitively open. He would have gone to the so-called bosom of Abraham to await the Redemption of the living and the dead. And it is perfectly plausible that he was one of those resurrected after the death of Jesus and to whom Matthew refers: "the earth quaked: the stones were split; the tombs opened and the bodies of many holy men rose from the dead, and these, after his resurrection, came out of the tombs, entered the Holy City and appeared to a number of people" (27:51-53). The founder of Opus Dei shares this idea, who, for example, preached in a meditation: "Think that Tradition tells us that St. Joseph died assisted by the Blessed Virgin and by our Lord. It is certain, because Sacred Scripture tells us, that when Christ came out of the tomb many just men were resurrected with Him, and went up with Him to Heaven. Isn't it logical that He should want to have by his side the one who had served as his father on earth?" [116].

---

116 Quoted by Lauretino Maria Herran, *La devoción de San Josemaría a san José*, Ed.Palabra II, 12.

Memento Mori

It is wise to reflect on our life and especially on our death. At times, it can be difficult and scary. But if it is done in the presence of God, as is typical of a retreat or a time of prayer, we should not be terribly scared. On the contrary, the benefit of such meditation is great. We are not immortal and we cannot look the other way, as if this fact had nothing to do with us. Someday our passage on earth will end. It is of the utmost importance that at that moment we should be in the right conditions to face death. But the preparation for it is not a matter of a few days or weeks. Of course, also those who assume that they will soon leave this world will have to accelerate this preparation. They say that Goethe's mother, already very ill, rejected an inopportune visit with an ironic reply: "The lady is very busy dying". The ideal is to prepare ourselves throughout life, because 'one dies as one lives'. And it is not only about how we would like to be remembered but, above all, strive to complete lovingly the task received from God.

Joseph, once heard from the angel: "do not be afraid" (cf. Mt 1:20). It is true that it was in a concrete context: do not be afraid to receive Mary, your wife. But God's frequent recommendation "do not be afraid" -also said to Mary, to the shepherds, to the apostles, to women after the Resurrection- also has to do with our existence. St. Josemaria used to repeat that one must live "without fear of life and without fear of death". Life is an adventure with many possibilities to work for God, to make use of the talents received, and ultimately, to be very happy. We should not be afraid to live because God is by our side and on our side. "I will be with you always: yes, to the end of time" (Mt 28:20).

It is worth living each day as if it were the last. Always trying to give our best answer. I don't know what I can do tomorrow, next week or in a few years if I'm still alive. But I do know that today I can try to make those around me happy. That God is waiting for me at work so that I can show my love, striving to do it well. That I can seek a constant presence of Jesus and Mary in everything I do.

In the Hail Mary we make allusions to two moments of time: "now" and "at the hour of our death". For both most decisive moments we ask the intercession of our Mother. For "now": asking that the reality of the present does not escape us. And for the most important moment of "our death": so that we, like St. Joseph, may be well accompanied, and that Our Lord finds us with hands full of fruit.

Someone has said to enter Heaven clean hands are not needed so much as full hands. Yes, let's try to be clean, to ask for forgiveness, but without forgetting that God expects us to bear fruit: "Every branch in me that bears no fruit he cuts away, and every branch that does bear fruit he prunes to make it bear even more… As a branch cannot bear fruit all by itself, but must remain part of the vine, neither can you unless you remain in me…Whoever remains in me, with me in him, bears fruit in plenty, for cut off from me you can do nothing... It is to the glory of my Father that you should bear much fruit and then you will be my disciples" (cf. Jn 15:1-8). Meditation on death, the awareness that time is short, serenely urges us not to fall asleep in a lukewarm or 'bourgeois' life, to make life productive, the life that has been given us.

Is death the end?

To illustrate what happens in the face of death. Mamerto Menapace compares it to what happens to babies at the time of their birth: "After nine months of gestation, the child senses that something is going to happen. The contractions announce it. Everything enters the strange situation of rupture and passage. Finally, delivery occurs for the mother who gives birth. But for the child the experience is very different. He feels that he is being expelled, forcing him to abandon the familiar place, the known place, the safe place. He knows nothing about the rest. If he could put it into words, perhaps he would say to himself in anguish: This is the end!

"His parents, and all those who await his coming, know very well that this is not the absolute end. It is simply the conclusion of a stage and the beginning of true life. It is true that in the womb there was no cold, nor hunger, nor were there social classes. But, at this stage, he does not fall into the void. A pair of paternal arms and maternal breasts await to receive him".

"This second stage will be immensely better. Neither the eye saw nor the ear heard in the mother's womb what was prepared for him when his parents could fully express their love face to face. It was nine months ago. Now it could be ninety years. Before it was only the time to grow by receiving. Now begins the time of sharing, growing together by giving and receiving. Stage of seeing, feeling, loving, communicating and giving life so that others may live"

Something similar happens to us as we grow up and "life announces that we are moving towards the anguish of a new stage. For those of us who groan in the womb of this earth, what will be beyond is incomprehensible and unimaginable. It happened to us when our own birth was approaching. When our second breakup approaches, it may be that we relive the old experience that we celebrate every birthday, but of which we remember only the joy of our parents. They were the ones who taught us to celebrate it. But, if we were sincere, we should know that it was what made us exclaim, just as it will now: This is the end!"

"Those who await our arrival will smile knowing that it is only a painful and festive beginning. Two fatherly arms await us and we hear: "Come, you whom my Father has blessed, take for your heritage the Kingdom prepared for you!".

"Life is not taken away from us, we are invited to live in a new stage" [117].

Death is not the definitive end. Far from being a door that closes, it is one that opens to a much better new life. It is hard for us to imagine it, just like the newborn who

117 *Cuentos rodados*, Editorial Patria Grande, cap. XXIII.

mistakenly feels that he is losing. But after death, a face to face encounter with God awaits the Christian, which entails complete happiness, without any mixture of evil, and forever. Heaven "also consists in the perfect satisfaction of our desires, since there the blessed will have more than what they wished or hoped for. The reason for this is because in this life no one can satisfy his desires, and no created thing can ever satiate the desire of man: only God can satisfy him, plentiful up to infinity" [118].

Patron of the Good Death

The *Catechism of the Catholic Church* assumes the tradition of calling St. Joseph "Patron of a happy death" and invites us to trust him [119]. Let's not wait until this trance be imminent to entrust ourselves to him. Let us count on his daily help to make us be worthy of the prize promised to the blessed, to those who love God. And let us also be diligent in helping relatives and friends to face this significant passage of our life.

Recently I have been very comforted hearing a friend say how he provided the means for a dying person to receive the last sacraments. The previous afternoon the chaplain of the hospital where the patient was admitted wanted to visit him, but a daughter and the cardiologist would not let him in because they did not want him to be "scared". Knowing about this, my friend went directly to speak to the sick person, he did it with the delicacy that his situation required and told him how important it would be to receive all possible help to face whatever was coming (the Anointing of the sick and the Eucharist). Needless to say, the patient accepted hopefully what was offered and joyfully received the sacraments.

118 S. Tomás, *Sobre el Credo,* 1, c. III.

119 N. 1014.

Since "To live in heaven is to be with Christ" [120], there is no doubt that Joseph had an advance here on earth. Although he did not see the glory of his Son in the style of what the apostles present at the Transfiguration of Jesus saw for some moments, he did participate in the day to day of his holiness and of his company. How much he enjoyed all that time! Even more because he was also next to the most holy creature, his beloved Spouse.

In addition, Joseph lived here such an anticipation of the eternal prize since, as has been said, heaven is the place where God's will is always fulfilled. The earth resembles or becomes heaven to the extent that this will is fulfilled, while it remains earth -the opposite of heaven- to the extent that it is subtracted to the divine will [121]. The Holy Patriarch lived close to Him who, upon entering this world, could say: "Here I come....to do, O God, your will" (Heb 10:7) and also close to her who received the praise of being blessed for doing the Father's will (cf. Mat 12: 46-50). And he himself lovingly spent his entire existence carrying out the divine designs. Therefore, as God is not outdone in generosity, He granted his humble house to be that little piece of heaven.

His life teaches us that, *mutatis mutandis*, we can live something similar. Whoever sincerely seeks the union with God through grace and to live in his presence, whoever allows the Lord and the Virgin Mary to enter his existence and is orientated towards the loving fulfillment of the divine will, can already have his share of heaven on earth. And the happiness achieved in this way, also ensures the eternal prize: "the happiness in Heaven is for those who know how to be happy on earth" [122]. It is what is gained by whoever is grateful for everything he has received, who does not complain about his luck and who lives making others happy.

---

120 *Cathecism of Chatolic Church*, n. 1028.

121 J.Ratzinger - Benedicto XVI, *Jesús de Nazareth II*, Planeta, Cap. II.

122 *Forge*, 1005.

Epilogue

Ite ad Joseph: Go to Joseph.
Genesis 41:55

At the end of these reflections on the life of the Holy Patriarch which have tried to follow the thread of the holy life of the faithful custodian of Jesus and Mary, we can accept as given to us the advice that Pharaoh gave his people, who were hungry as a result of a great drought: "Go to Joseph and do whatever he tells you!".

That Joseph of the Old Testament, whose story is told with great skill and ability to attract attention in Genesis chapters 37 to 47, is a figure of Jesus Christ, but he is also a figure of our Joseph of the New Testament. With admirable synthesis St. Bernard teaches it: "That Joseph sold because of the envy of his brothers and led into Egypt, forecast that Christ would be sold: this other Joseph, fleeing from the envy of Herod took Christ into Egypt. That one due to fidelity to his Lord did not want to unite himself to the woman; this one recognizing his wife as a virgin mother of his Lord and keeping continence, faithfully protected her. That one was to understand the mysteries of dreams, this one was to be knowledgeable and participated in the heavenly sacraments. That one kept wheat, not for himself, but for all the people; this one was commissioned to take care of the living bread that comes down from heaven, both for himself and for the whole world"[123].

Joseph was great: whenever we approach his life, we are confirmed in this reality. He is the holiest man. Someone who from silence and humility reached high levels of holiness. "And so it was that a simple, hard-working, patient, long-suffering, helpful, quiet, humble, obedient and ignored

123 *Homiliae super Missus est*, 2,16

man was praised as a just, faithful, prudent and good man; as an effective man, who knew how to get ahead in difficult circumstances with the family that God placed in his care, protecting them from dangers and liberating them"[124].

In addition to being a great advocate, he is an approachable model. He is not a martyr who offers his life in a way that we consider far from our daily realities. He is not an inimitable apostle who tirelessly traveled the world. He is not wise in a human manner who dazzled everyone with his research and teachings. "Joseph, a simple man, searched for God; Joseph a detached man, found God, Joseph a retired man enjoyed God"[125].

"If you want my advice, which I have never tired of repeating these many years, *Ite ad Joseph*: "Go to St. Joseph". He will show us definite ways, both human and divine, to approach Jesus"[126]. These meditations were mainly intended to help during a few days of retreat and moments of prayer. In any case I personally propose to the reader, what I propose to myself as I end these pages: go more often to St. Joseph. How? As the Holy Spirit let us understand, but perhaps it can be like this:

- ask him for help at every prayer time, at the beginning and the end;
- count on his intercession as we prepare for Holy Mass and as we give thanks at the end;
- offer our work through him and carry it out as holy as possible;
- entrust to him the spiritual life of our relatives and friends;
- go to the "patron of the happy death" when we hear of someone dying;

124 *Joseph, Mary's husband*, p. 278.

125 Bossuet, *Segundo panegírico de San José*, citado por F. F. Carvajal, *Hablar con Dios*, 2° domingo de San José.

126 *Christ is passing by*, 38.

- keep him present when saying the Rosary;
- remember him on Wednesdays;
- keep him as a reference of fidelity to our own vocation.

God willing that we have grown in affection towards Joseph and by his hand, also towards Jesus and Mary. *Jesus, Mary and Joseph, make me always be with you three!*

www.ingramcontent.com/pod-product-compliance
Ingram Content Group UK Ltd.
Pitfield, Milton Keynes, MK11 3LW, UK
UKHW021915190726
13853UKWH00002B/685